Dancing as a Career for Men

Richard Glasstone

Photography by Simon Rae-Scott

Sterling Publishing Co., Inc. New York

Originally published in Great Britain under the title, 'Male Dancing as a Career.' Copyright © Kaye & Ward Ltd 1980
American edition first published in 1981 by
Sterling Publishing Co., Inc.
Two Park Avenue
New York, N.Y. 10016

All rights reserved. No part of this publication may be reproduced, stored in a retrieval system, or transmitted, in any form or by any means, electronic, mechanical, photocopying, recording or otherwise, without the prior permission of the copyright owner.
Library of Congress Catalog Card No.: 80-54339
Sterling ISBN 0-8069-4640-7 Trade
                  4641-5 Library
Manufactured in the United States of America

CONTENTS

Foreword by Anthony Dowell		vii
Acknowledgements		ix
1	Practical Advice For the Aspiring Young Dancer and his Parents	1
2	The Dancing Male	9
3	Ballet	19
4	Modern or Contemporary Dance	35
5	Showbusiness	49
6	The Partner	61
7	Working Conditions and Career Prospects	74
8	A Day in the Life of a Professional Dancer	79
9	Dancing for Pleasure; Educational Dance; and Dance as Therapy or as an Aid to Sport	89
10	Directory of Practical Information and Useful Addresses	97

FOR NORA ROCHE
WHO HAS TAUGHT ME SO MUCH
ABOUT TEACHING DANCE
Richard Glasstone

FOREWORD

For a young boy to make up his mind whether he is sufficiently determined to become a dancer is no easy matter. Nor is it easy for his parents to advise him, or even to decide whether they think that the boy is certain that this is what he really wants to do.

In this very down to earth book Richard Glasstone sets out briefly, but very comprehensively, to help both boy and parents. He deals with all forms of dance, and I am especially glad to see that he encourages young dancers to study more than one form of dance, while specializing in their own particular choice.

Mr Glasstone does not try to hide the hardness of the training, nor the courage that is often needed to persevere.

I started to dance at a much earlier age than Mr Glasstone recommends. But for those starting later — and they are the great majority — I think that this book will help them to decide whether to start, and whether to continue with a career which I, for one, have found greatly rewarding but very hard work.

ACKNOWLEDGEMENTS

The author wishes to thank the numerous colleagues, students and friends who have helped in so many different ways in the preparation of this book, as well as the directors and staff of the numerous schools and other specialist organizations who have so generously provided information and assistance. Special thanks are due to all the dancers who kindly posed for the photographs and also to the following people for their invaluable help and advice: Anthony Dowell, David Wall, Barbara Fewster, Helen Kastrati, Norman Morrice, Peter Wright, Robert Cohan, Charles Augins, Shiela Darby, Olga Fricker, Joe Yanello, Sharon Romeyko, Lucille McLure, Arnette Zerbe, Jonathan Burrows, David Leonard, Karel Poons, Betty Oliphant, Natasha Lisakova, Colin Fleming, Stephen Sheriff, Mary Clarke, Ava Loiacono, Mrs M. I. Jack, Mr G. B. L. Wilson and last but not least Heather Glasstone.

The excerpt from Saint-Hubert's 'How to compose successful ballets' from *Dance as a theatre art* edited by Selma Jeanne Cohen, is reprinted by kind permission of the publishers, Dance Books Ltd.

The photograph of students of the National Ballet School of Canada is by Jeannette Edessi Collins.

1

PRACTICAL ADVICE
FOR THE ASPIRING YOUNG DANCER
AND HIS PARENTS

There are promising career prospects nowadays for good male dancers. Interesting, and in many cases financially secure job opportunities exist in a number of fields, ranging from classical ballet to showbusiness and contemporary dance. But in spite of the fact that so many men all over the world now dance professionally, there is still prejudice against male dancers. This book hopes to demonstrate that dancing can be a viable and socially acceptable career for men, and to show that there is nothing effeminate about good male dancing.

Contrary to popular belief, it is unnecessary for dancers to start their training in early childhood. Much depends on the type of dancing to be studied, but even for a career in classical ballet (for which one does need to start fairly early), training in earnest need not commence before the boy is ten or eleven years old; and to start ballet training before the age of eight could be positively harmful. A younger child's knees are not yet strong enough to be trained balletically, and the bones of the foot are still too soft. Furthermore, ballet is a highly sophisticated, essentially adult concept of movement; the very young child would derive greater benefit, as well as more enjoyment, from a less imitative and less physically demanding type of dancing.

Most young boys develop at a slower rate than girls of an equivalent age. So, in some ways, it can be a good idea to wait until the boy is twelve or thirteen years old before embarking on full-time professional training. By then, not only is the pattern of his physical development more predictable, but the decision to dance can also be more of a conscious commitment on his part, rather than being something his parents have encouraged him to do.

What about the late beginner who wants to have a career in dance? Much will depend on his physique, but provided his body is sufficiently supple, it is possible (but by no means easy) for a young man to start training in his late teens or exceptionally, in his early twenties and — with a great deal of hard, concentrated work — still become sufficiently accomplished to dance professionally.

Much depends on whether he wants to be a classical ballet dancer, a modern dancer, or whether he is aiming for a career in showbusiness. There are three separate chapters dealing, in turn, with each of these three main categories; they will give the reader more detailed information about the specific requirements for each of these types of dance.

There is nowadays a tendency in dancing (as in many other fields) to specialize too much, and too soon. To achieve excellence in any particular style of movement will, of course, require a long period of concentrated, specialized study; but this need not preclude all work in other styles. There is no reason at all, for instance, why an aspiring ballet dancer should not learn a little jazz or tap dancing, or why the committed modern dancer should not increase his range by taking some classical ballet classes. Done in moderation, no one type of dance is harmful or antagonistic to another: on the contrary, a degree of versatility can be highly beneficial.

Having decided to take dancing lessons, the next step is choosing where to study. Most children start locally. Many countries, including Britain and the U.S.A., still have no state licensing system for dance teachers, but many teachers are accredited to professional organizations. Among the best known are the Imperial Society of Teachers of Dancing (of which the Cecchetti Society is a branch), the Royal Academy of Dancing (R.A.D.) and the British Ballet Organization (B.B.O.). These are international bodies, with headquarters in London.

Some organizations deal with only one type of dance; others, like the Imperial Society of Teachers of Dancing (known as the I.S.T.D.) are very comprehensive. The I.S.T.D. is divided into two faculties. All stage branches are covered by the Theatre Faculty; these include classical ballet (Cecchetti and I.S.T.D. methods), tap dancing and modern stage dancing (musical comedy and jazz work), national dance, historical dance, and revived Greek

Practical Advice for the Aspiring Young Dancer

dance. Then there is the Ballroom Faculty, covering most forms of social dancing. All these branches hold tests and examinations regularly, in various different categories (for amateurs, students, professionals and teachers), in the United Kingdom and several European countries, as well as in the U.S.A., Canada, South Africa, Australia and New Zealand. Headquarters should be able to put prospective pupils in touch with a teacher in their own area. Another way of finding a teacher is by consulting one of the specialist dance publications. *The Dancing Times* and, to a lesser degree, *Dance and Dancers* (both published monthly in London), list dancing schools throughout Britain, and *Dance Magazine* (published monthly in New York) does the same for the U.S.A. These magazines also carry advertisements for schools in many other countries.

Local dancing teachers ought to be able to recognize potential talent. Generally speaking, they will be able to recommend whether a pupil should audition for a professional dancing school and will help him to go about this. Unfortunately, there are some teachers who are reluctant, for one reason or another, to see their pupils move on to the big professional schools. If a boy feels that he is being held back or, indeed, if there is no dancing school in his area, it is always possible to apply direct to one of the professional schools for an audition. It is better to have had some training beforehand, but most professional schools would prefer a student with no training at all to one who has been over-trained.

Some schools, like the Royal Ballet Lower School (at White Lodge, near London) offer full-time dance training combined with secondary education and boarding facilities, for children aged eleven to sixteen. Others, like the London School of Contemporary Dance, or the senior section of the Royal Ballet School, cater to graduates wanting a full-time professional dance training. The former concentrates specifically on modern dance, the latter on classical ballet. Each includes some classes in the other discipline, as is nowadays the norm, but they are essentially specialist schools. There are other schools geared to giving a much broader-based training, including tap and jazz, as well as drama — these are often referred to as stage schools. The addresses of a number of professional schools of different types are listed in the Directory. Some are day schools, others residential. Further information can be obtained by writing to the principal of the school concerned.

If a boy or a young man is sufficiently promising to pass an audition at one of the major professional schools, there should be no real problem about fees. Various grants are available at either government or local authority level and many schools and organizations offer scholarships and bursaries, in particular to promising male dancers. Circumstances vary from one area to another, and the school where the boy auditions will advise him as to the possibilities available locally. But the real enthusiast will never be deterred by lack of money. Many a good dancer has worked his way through dancing school or taken on part-time work of some kind to help finance his studies. If a boy really wants to dance, and his teachers say he has sufficient talent and physical facility, he shouldn't let anything or anyone stop him from trying.

Talent is an indefinable quality, and it should not be confused with physical facility. To have the latter means that one has the right kind of body for a dancer: free moving joints, a strong but supple back, flexible feet, well-proportioned limbs, and, for classical ballet, legs that turn out freely in the hip socket. It can also mean things like having a good natural jump and sense of turn, and an ability to keep time to the music. Talent is more to do with the way a dancer moves, how he phrases his movements, how he projects his personality and, above all, how he is able to convey, through movement, an innate understanding of the mood or the meaning of the choreography he is dancing. Some talented artists lack the physical facility that would enable them to exploit their potential to the full; but where there is real talent, determination and hard work can sometimes achieve miracles. Yet all the physical facility in the world cannot make an artist out of the dancer without real talent.

The dance publications mentioned above carry advertisements for specialist suppliers of dancing shoes, tights, leotards, jazz pants, dance supports, castanets, taps and everything else the student requires in the way of equipment. The addresses of these and of other similar publications, as well as of numerous companies, schools and other relevant organizations, will also be found in the Directory.

Beginners would be well advised not to buy dancing shoes or any other practice clothing without first consulting their prospective school or teacher. Apart from the fact that some schools require specific dance uniforms to be worn, specialist advice and help are necessary, particularly when fitting

Practical Advice for the Aspiring Young Dancer

ballet shoes for the first time.

Modern dance classes are done barefoot; for most other types of dancing class some special kind of footwear will be needed, such as ballet shoes (soft toe — males don't dance on *pointe*, except as a gimmick), character shoes or boots, tap shoes, jazz shoes, etc. Prices vary, but the cost of a pair of jazz shoes, for instance, is comparable to that of a good pair of leather walking shoes; ballet shoes are rather less expensive. But whereas many young men simply wear ordinary canvas shoes (plimsolls or sneakers) for jazz classes, for a ballet class it really is essential to wear the correct shoes.

Jeans and a tee-shirt are often what men wear for a jazz class, but special jazz pants are available and lightweight tracksuits or jumpsuits are also popular for this kind of work. For ballet, dancers need tights (very young boys sometimes wear shorts or swimming trunks) and most contemporary-style dancers also wear tights for training. A special dance support (or jock belt) is always worn under tights; indeed, it is advisable for male dancers always to wear a support, for all types of dancing. Tights can be purchased with or without feet (the latter are usually worn for class work, often with socks) and they are held up either by rolling the top end around a belt or an elastic band round the waist, or else with broad elastic bands worn, like braces, over the shoulders. The tights (which can be made of wool or cotton, but are nowadays usually nylon or lycra) can be worn with a leotard made out of the same sort of stretchy, form-fitting fabric, or the whole garment may be all-in-one body-tights. Instead of a leotard, many dancers wear a tee-shirt, singlet or some other type of comfortable top. Prices vary a great deal and it is a good idea to get two or three specialist suppliers to send their catalogues. When choosing practice clothes two things should be remembered: they will need to be easily washable (dancers do a lot of perspiring!) and should keep the pupil warm, but not so cluttered that the teacher cannot see clearly how his muscles are working.

As previously stated, examinations are conducted in various types of dancing by the I.S.T.D. Another important dance organization which also conducts examinations (but only in classical ballet) is The Royal Academy of Dancing (R.A.D.). And there are others (see Directory). In some ways, working towards these examinations can be beneficial to the young student. For instance, he will be striving towards achieving a specific level of execution in a given period of time; and an examiner's impartial comments

5

on the standard achieved can be a useful guide for further study. My own advice to pupils taking a dance examination is always to try and think of it as if it were a performance. In the theatre, when the curtain goes up, dancers have to try and perform at their best, regardless of the circumstances. The same is true of an examination. But one must not over-estimate the importance of dance examinations. Indeed, there is absolutely no need ever to have taken an examination set by an examining body like the R.A.D., the B.B.O. or the I.S.T.D. in order to get into a professional company. A few ballet companies draw their dancers exclusively from the ranks of their own schools, and hold their own, internal examinations (e.g. the Paris Opera Ballet); but most companies with their own schools will also audition dancers from outside the organization. Many companies have no school of their own and hold regular auditions once or twice a year (or whenever a vacancy occurs); these are advertised in the dance press and, sometimes, on the notice boards of the larger dance studios. In normal circumstances, a ballet student's training will be nearing completion and he will be ready to start attending auditions by the age of eighteen or nineteen. To get into a company or a show, a dancer needs to be successful at one of these auditions; success or failure in dance examinations forms no part of this selection process. For free-lance dancers, like most people in showbusiness, attending auditions is part and parcel of their professional lives, as was so vividly illustrated in the musical show *A Chorus Line*. Learning to cope with the pressures of dance examinations as a student could be a useful preparation for this kind of situation later on.

    It is of even greater value (indeed, I believe it is essential) for the child or student, from time to time, to get some sort of performing experience — if possible in a theatre. The local school's annual display, the occasional dance competition — anything like this is good experience, so long as it is done in moderation. Children who are allowed to perform in public too frequently, particularly in competition work, all too often find their talent fading by the time they reach their late teens.

    As explained above, some professional schools provide full-time secondary education in conjunction with dance studies. Where this is not available, as the child grows older, combining schoolwork with the demands of daily dancing lessons can become increasingly difficult. As the young student becomes more and more skilled at his dancing, and as his dancing begins to make ever-increasing demands on his time and his energies, he may tend to neglect his schoolwork, regarding much of it as irrelevant to his chosen profession. This is something which really must not be encouraged. A dancer's career is a short one. The options available after his active career as a dancer comes to a close are discussed in the chapter 'Working Conditions and Career Prospects', but whatever he does, he will need the benefit of as good an education as he can get.

He must, of course, face the possibility of physical injury which might entail having to retrain for another career, but quite apart from being an insurance against any such misfortune, a good, all-round education is an asset to any dancer. He need not be an intellectual or an academic (in fact, the temperament of the academically gifted child is often incompatible with the needs of a theatrical performer) but he must have an active mind and a sensitive understanding of musical, historical and artistic style.

Musical training is particularly important. Dalcroze eurhythmics are an excellent introduction to music and movement for any child, and learning to sing and to play a musical instrument are valuable experiences for all dancers. But a dancer is an athlete as well as an artist; he must learn to understand and to take care of his own body. A detailed knowledge of anatomy is not necessary. Simple common sense plays an important part in keeping him fit and injury free. A dancer must do regular, daily classes. He must learn to differentiate between the routine muscular aches that are a dancer's lot, and those pains, especially in the knees and lower-back, which could herald potential injury. He must never jump or do any other strenuous movement unless all the muscles are warm. This means not only doing warming-up exercises beforehand, but also maintaining the muscles in a state of readiness throughout a long rehearsal, particularly if it entails lengthy periods of inactivity. Diets are not necessary and can be dangerous. They should only be undertaken on medical advice and under expert supervision. If a dancer eats well, gets lots of sleep, and keeps any drinking or smoking to a minimum, then the sheer hard work of regular dancing classes should keep him as fit as any man could wish to be.

In conclusion I would say that unless a boy is very determined that he really does want to dance more than anything else in the world, he should not think of taking it up seriously. On the other hand, if he feels deeply that this is his vocation, nothing should be allowed to dissuade him from trying.

If he does not succeed as a dancer, or if he finds in the end that it's not what he really wanted after all, he will still be young enough to change course. The mental and physical discipline he will have acquired in the process can only stand him in good stead for the future; but if he delays in starting, it may well be too late to change his mind at a future date.

2

THE DANCING MALE

Historically, men have always danced. The role of the male, and often his predominance in tribal and folk dance, is taken for granted. From the days of court dancing, via ballroom to present-day disco, dancing — in the social context — has always been a perfectly natural male pursuit. Why then, when it is transferred to the stage, has the dance (particularly ballet) sometimes come to be regarded as an unsuitable occupation for a man? To understand this issue we need to examine it in both its social and its historical perspective.

Is Male Dancing Effeminate?

Many people have an idea that there is something effeminate about male dancing. This varies from vague notions about men looking 'silly' in tights, or a feeling that it's somehow 'soft' for men to dance, to a conviction that most male dancers are homosexuals.

This is not the place to pass value judgements on homosexuality. It exists, and there are homosexuals in every walk of life. Dancers, like many theatrical people, are less secretive about such matters than some sections of society, but this does not mean that the incidence of homosexuality is higher in the theatre.

There are people for whom these concerns seem to be tied up with the general image they have of all artists and theatre folk as immoral and dissolute members of society. But dancers are athletes; without strong, healthy bodies they could not do their physically very demanding work. No dancer can afford to indulge in drink or drugs. As to morality, sexual or otherwise, surely this is a matter of upbringing and personal conviction, rather than of choice of profession? There is no way dancing as such can make anyone into a homosexual.

Effeminate behaviour and homosexuality do frequently go together; but they are often two separate, unconnected issues. Some boys are effeminate by nature, without being homosexual. Others may acquire effeminate mannerisms by imitation and association; but like affectations of any kind, they are deplored and rejected by all good artists. Any boy or man who dances like a girl or a woman is not a good dancer. Effeminate male dancing is quite simply bad dancing.

In an age which glorifies sport, it is ironical that the male dancer — who can vie with any athlete or sportsman in physical agility, as well as in sheer strength and stamina — should sometimes be looked down on as being 'soft'.

The whole question of what we regard as masculine jobs, manly behaviour, or a suitably masculine appearance — as, indeed of what we look upon as feminine occupations, behaviour and dress — is a very complex one. It reflects the attitudes, prejudices and taboos of different nations and of different social classes, the emphasis often shifting subtly from generation to generation. For instance, many of us can remember the days when long hair was considered 'cissy', or at best 'hippy' — until footballers started to grow theirs, making it an acceptably masculine fashion in the eyes of many who had previously despised it.

The way we feel and think about ourselves and about the society in which we live, affects the way we dress and behave; this is reflected in the way we dance — both socially and on stage or screen. The twentieth century revolution in sexual attitudes has resulted in a blurring of many of the old dividing lines between the sexes. Just as young men and women now often dress alike in identical jeans and sweaters, so do male and female dancers wear almost identical tights and leotards; the once so distinctive frills and flounces of the ballerina are fast acquiring a period flavour.

Both modern ballet and contemporary dance reflect the athleticism, as well as the uninhibited sexuality of today's world; the popular image of the ballerina as the fairy on the top of the Christmas tree is at last beginning to fade, and with it the stereotyped image of the male ballet dancer as an effete, mannered creature whose only real purpose is to support her.

The Dancing Male

The male dancer used to be ridiculed as a music-hall joke. For a time he was merely accepted as a necessary evil. The almost pop star adulation enjoyed in recent years by artists like Nureyev and Baryshnikov, is one of the most remarkable changes to have occurred in our theatre in recent years. But what many people do not realize is that the status now being accorded to male dancers is not so much an innovation as a return to the state of affairs which existed in Western Europe before the nineteenth century.

The Male Dancer in History

It has been said that the history of ballet is the history of the male dancer and in the eighteenth century we find, in Western Europe, a veritable galaxy of male talent: not only gifted dancers like the famous Dupré — known as 'the Great' — and Vestris, whom his fans called 'the God of the Dance', but also talented choreographers and brilliant theoreticians and teachers, such as Weaver (in England), Noverre (in France and in Stuttgart), Dauberval (also in France) and Vigano (in Italy). As late as 1781, we are told that a sitting of Parliament was suspended to allow members to attend a performance, in London, by the legendary father and son, Gaetano and Auguste Vestris, the greatest French dancers of the period. In our day not even Nureyev has been accorded quite that degree of recognition!

Why was it, then, that male dancing was later to fall into such disrepute?

The rot began to set in when women first started dancing *sur les pointes*, on the tips of their toes. This was in the early nineteenth century, a time when the fashion in literature and the arts was to idealize woman as an unattainable, often exotic creature. By rising on her *pointes*, dressed in flimsy tulle skirts, the ballerina added to the air of otherworldliness so much admired at the time. The male, on the other hand, found himself cast in the role of the doomed, lovelorn poet, worshipping at the shrine of the elusive, unattainable female.

At its best, this Romantic convention produced great ballets like *Giselle*, but as the convention hardened into a stereotyped formula, the function of the male dancer became more and more that of a mere support for the dainty, ethereal ballerina, until most men no longer wanted to be associated with what was fast becoming a decadent and marginal art form — and the public had little regard for those who were.

As ballet in Western Europe reached its lowest ebb, men's roles were even taken by women *en travesti*. A sad state of affairs indeed for the male dancer who, in some respects, could trace his lineage back to the court of Versailles, where King Louis XIV of France himself had danced leading roles in many court ballets. Of course these lavish entertainments of the nobility were very different from what we today call ballet, but they were to some extent the root from which that later form of theatre was to grow. To understand the role of the male in the development of theatre dance we need to look at how dance as a form of entertainment evolved out of social dance.

Dance as a Social Pastime

Social dance (as distinct from folk dance) had developed at the European courts from the simple forms of the mediaeval couple dance to the complex technique and elaborate etiquette of the court dances of the sixteenth, seventeenth and eighteenth centuries.

These were essentially the dance of one man with one woman, whether performed by one or several couples at a time. Dancing was considered to be an essential part of every nobleman's education — witness this quotation from a dance manual by St Hubert, published in Paris in 1641:

'Everyone knows that for a young nobleman to be polished he must learn how to ride, to fence and to dance. The first skill increases his dexterity, the second his courage, the last his grace and disposition. Each of these exercises being useful at the appropriate time, one can say that they are of equal value, since Mars is no less the god of war when resting on Venus' bosom than when thundering in the midst of battles.'

So we have riding, fencing and dancing as desirable social accomplishments for a seventeenth century nobleman. Are they so very different from those desired by a young man of today; to drive a car, to be able to hold his own in a fight (or a football match) and to shine at the disco? But there is one big difference. Nowadays we live in a society where many barriers have been broken down; barriers between the sexes, but even more to the point, the old dividing lines of class. It has become difficult for young people of this generation to understand the paramount importance of the class system in earlier societies. The way people thought, dressed ... and *danced* was very much dictated by the social class to which they belonged; the kind of dancing done at court was the exclusive prerogative of the nobility.

Peasants and other working people had their own, more robust way of dancing: a number of these dances has survived as part of the rich tradition of European folk dance, and some were refined and stylized as they were gradually incorporated into the dances of the nobility.

It was some time before the middle classes began to emerge as an important section of society; as they slowly gained in affluence and power, they were to adopt more and more those social pastimes and pleasures formerly enjoyed only by the nobility: little by little, court dancing was to evolve into the kind of social dancing that would later become the ballroom dancing of the nineteenth and early twentieth centuries. But court dancing had also developed along another line, as an essential ingredient of the lavish court entertainments of the sixteenth, seventeenth and eighteenth centuries.

Dance as an Entertainment at the European Courts

In addition to the balls given at court and in the great houses, dancing also played an important role in court entertainments such as the elaborate French 'ballets de cour' in which, as we have seen, the King of France himself danced the leading roles. These court ballets were not performed on a raised stage, but in the central areas of great halls, with the audience of courtiers seated on three sides. The important thing to remember is that the dancers were not professional performers. Professional dancing masters were employed to coach them, and to mount the spectacles but, initially, both performers and audience consisted exclusively of the nobility. The relationship between audience and performer was thus very different from the one existing nowadays at a ballet performance.

How many men in a present-day ballet audience have ever had any personal, physical experience of the type of movement they are watching? Yet the dance technique used in court ballets was essentially that of the social dances in which every nobleman was schooled. As he sat watching his peers perform, he was thus able to experience a genuinely physical recognition of the movements he saw. This so-called kinaesthetic sympathy created a bond between audience and performer. This was gradually lost as the professionals later took over from the courtiers, and the dancers' skills became more and more specialized and acrobatic, to satisfy the demands of the growing middle-class public of the commercial theatre. To their own, more earthy heritage of tricks and grotesque dancing, the professionals (mainly strolling players, tumblers, acrobats and buffoons) began to add the refinements of the noble style which they had not previously been allowed to learn; it was out of this amalgamation that the theatrical form of dancing we now call ballet gradually evolved.

The gulf between the kind of dancing which fell within the personal experience of the average member of a theatre audience, and that performed on stage, widened irrevocably; dance was on its way to becoming a highly specialized performance art. By the time of the French Revolution (1789), ballet had long shed its courtly connections and was firmly established as a commercial entertainment frequented by the emerging middle classes.

Female dancers were still very much encumbered by the heavy costumes of the period, and although significant costume reforms took place during the course of the eighteenth century, it was some time before these were such as to give the women sufficient freedom of movement to enable them to compete on more equal terms with the growing technical virtuosity of the men.

Back in 1670, when he retired from performing, King Louis XIV of France had established the institution which — with various changes of name under different regimes — was to evolve into the ballet school and company of the Paris Opera. At first all the dancers were men, and it was not until 1681 that women first appeared in public on the professional ballet stage in Paris. Less than two hundred years later the situation had become almost reversed with, as we have seen, women taking the men's roles in many ballets.

The Great Russian Revival

By about 1865, ballet in Western Europe was entering its most decadent phase. Denmark alone preserved its heritage of strong male dancing (thanks to the influence of its great choreographer, Bournonville), but the best French and Italian dancing masters had found work in Russia where the art

The Dancing Male

of ballet had begun to flourish at the court of the Czars. Here the skill and virility of the male dancer were still appreciated.

There had always been a strong tradition of male folk dancing in Slav countries, so it was considered very natural for men to dance. But there is another factor which is sometimes overlooked; the ballet in Czarist Russia was, in a way, still much closer to its ancient roots, a court entertainment in which the nobility had once taken part. To be sure, the dancers were by now all professional performers, but they were very much the *Imperial* Russian Ballet, the Czar's personal troupe. Seen against this background, their courtly bearing and refined manners must have carried a conviction no longer possible in the commercial ballet world of Western Europe, where such dignity and elegance had gradually degenerated into the superficial airs and graces of pantomime princes. The presence of two great male teachers, Cecchetti and Johansson, was another important factor in the preservation of high standards of male dancing in Russia in the latter part of the nineteenth century.

It was the Russian Imperial Ballet which, towards the end of the century, gave us the great Tchaikowsky ballets that still form the backbone of today's classical repertoire. Then, in 1909, Diaghilev brought his newly formed Ballets Russes to Paris for their first season. This company, initially made up of dancers from the Imperial Russian Ballet, was to revolutionize the art of ballet throughout the Western world. Two of its leading dancers, the legendary Pavlova and Nijinsky, were to become, in very different ways, the symbols of that revolution. As too, in another respect, were the company's choreographer, Fokine, and its other leading dancer, Karsavina.

Fokine insisted on dramatic and choreographic unity, raising ballet to new heights as a serious art form in its own right, with the male again occupying his proper place. Karsavina was Fokine's ideal ballerina, but it was her partner, Nijinksy, who stole the limelight and created a sensation at that first Paris season. Western Europe had forgotten the thrill and excitement of great male dancing and Nijinsky, with his phenomenal leaps, his dramatic intensity and the sensuous virility of his movement, initiated a whole new era of male dancing.

However, Nijinsky's work was seen only by the élite audience who attended performances of the Diaghilev Company. His co-star, the great Anna Pavlova, had left after the first season to form her own company. She toured the world, reaching a very much wider audience, and although she had several good partners, it was her solos, like the Dying Swan, which made the biggest impact, re-enforcing in the minds of the general public the image of the ballet dancer as an essentially delicate, feminine creature. Thousands of little girls wanted to emulate her and ballet schools sprang up everywhere in the wake of her world tours.

Twentieth Century Developments

Meanwhile, in other areas, dance as a serious art form continued to develop rapidly, and the importance of the male gradually came to be recognized more and more. The emergence and evolution of the various streams of modern dance, mainly in Germany and the U.S.A., contributed significantly to the consolidation of dance as a serious and respected theatre art. This so-called 'New Dance' encompassed and emphasized many different elements — naturalism, expressionism, athleticism — broadening choreographic horizons and creating fresh opportunities for the male. Between 1933 and 1940, Ted Shawn even toured the U.S.A., with an all-male company, doing much to re-establish the acceptance of the male dancer. At the same time Leonide Massine (who had been Nijinsky's successor with the Diaghilev Company), continued to dazzle the dance world with his brilliant character creations.

Yet it was to take the advent of two more Russian male classical ballet dancers to bring home to Western audiences the full potential of the male dancer. First of all Rudolf Nureyev, who in 1961 defected from Russia in a blaze of publicity. His magnificent dancing set new standards for our men and they rose splendidly to the challenge. He was followed in 1974 by Mikhail Baryshnikov, who made the sort of impact on American ballet that Nureyev had first made in Europe.

Not only had ballet audiences now grown to numbers unimaginable in Nijinsky's day, but thanks to the cinema and television, Nureyev and Baryshnikov were also able to reach a much bigger cross-section of society, showing the man in the street the excitement of really good male dancing.

The cinema has been a potent force in the popularization of the dance; first Fred Astaire and later Gene Kelly became household names and, more recently, John Travolta.

The Dancing Male

In Travolta the youth of the late seventies found a dance hero with whom they were able to identify. Most young men who watched his films tried to emulate him at their local disco. When they watched him dance on the screen, the audience could experience a genuinely physical recognition of his movements, thus creating a much closer bond between Travolta and his young fans than that which exists between the average member of a ballet audience (who has never learnt any ballet) and the professionals he sees performing on stage.

In some ways this bond, this kinaesthetic sympathy between Travolta and his audience, can be compared with that which united performers and onlookers at a seventeenth century performance of a court ballet, all of whom were nobles, and therefore themselves skilled dancers to a man.

So we would seem to have come full circle. Clearly dancing is a natural form of expression for both men and women. So long as it reflects the mood and the aspirations of a given generation in a given society, it can easily be translated into terms of theatre without affectation or emasculation. It is only when audiences cannot relate to what is happening on the stage that they become alienated. That does not diminish the validity of what is being performed, but it does imply a need for more education and better preparation on the part of both performers and spectators.

Phillip Broomhead, a graduate student at the Royal Ballet School.

3

BALLET

Books about ballet often tell us that there were two main schools of classical ballet: the French, notable for its grace and elegance and the Italian, excelling in strength and virtuosity; and that the two merged to form the Russian School. There is, of course, a very real basis of historical truth in this, but it is also, in many ways, something of an over-simplification. In any case, ballet is now so international, and there has been so much cross-fertilization that today these categories are often irrelevant.

That is not to say that ballet is taught in exactly the same way in England and America, or in France and Russia; there are a number of important differences in emphasis and approach, but the basic technique of ballet is like a universal language. In its academic, classroom form, this language is the same all over the world, but spoken, as it were, in a variety of accents. Everyone also uses the same French terminology; this has obvious practical advantages. A ballet dancer can follow the basic instructions given in a ballet class anywhere in the world; in fact, the names of some movements, such as *plié* (a bend of the knees), are borrowed from ballet terminology by many modern and jazz dancers.

The technique of ballet is founded on the principle that the legs and feet are fully turned outwards, ideally at an angle of ninety degrees. There are anatomical and aesthetic reasons for this; for example, by rotating the leg outwards in the hip socket, the dancer is able to raise it freely without altering the alignment of the hips.

There are five positions of the feet in classical ballet. They form the basis of the whole technique; academically, all the movements begin and end either in one of these five positions or in a position derived from one of them. There are rules governing the positioning and movement of the arms and the head. In part, these rules are dictated by the aesthetics of formal harmony, but they are also firmly rooted in the natural and logical laws of balance and opposition. The origins of some aspects of ballet technique are to be found in French and Italian court dancing, but this technique did not crystallize into its present form until the early nineteenth century, when it was codified by Carlo Blasis.

All choreographers working in the ballet idiom start off with dancers schooled in these academic principles of classical dance, the so-called *danse d'école*, but each choreographer uses his dancers' skills in his own, personal way, moulding the basic classical movements and steps into his own choreographic style.

The choreographer is to dance what the composer is to music. His work involves planning the structure of a dance or a ballet, as well as determining the movements to be performed by the dancers and their positioning on the stage; he devises their entrances, exits and groupings, and the patterns they make as they move, and it is he who dictates the relationship of the dance to the music. Whereas the term 'dance arrangement' describes only the skill of re-arranging conventional steps and movements in various ways (a skill possessed in some degree by any experienced dancing teacher), choreography implies a much more creative and original handling of movement; and besides creative talent, it also involves the skills of directing the rehearsals, moulding the interpretation and supervising the staging of a new work.

Choreographically, ballet encompasses a wide variety of styles, from the late nineteenth century classicism of *The Sleeping Beauty* or the earlier romanticism of *Giselle*, to the sparse, twentieth century athleticism of Balanchine's *Agon*, the stylized drama of De Valois' *Checkmate*, the lyricism of Ashton's *Symphonic Variations*, or the demi-character comedy of Cranko's *Pineapple Poll*.

Some ballet companies have a repertoire consisting mainly of works created especially for them, either by a succession of guest choreographers, or by their own resident one. Other companies perform a mixture of new ballets and established classics.

The New York City Ballet, for instance, has been almost exclusively the creative instrument of one man, George Balanchine, although numerous works by Jerome Robbins have enriched its programmes in recent years.

Ballet

The repertoire of the Royal Ballet, on the other hand, is founded on the full-length Petipa-Tchaikowsky classics, with a representative selection of one-act ballets from the Diaghilev repertoire. To these, new works by the Royal Ballet's own resident choreographers are added regularly. In addition to these works by Ashton and MacMillan, the repertoire also includes ballets by many other leading artists.

A similar pattern is followed by the American Ballet Theatre, the Australian Ballet and the Canadian National and Dutch National Ballet Companies.

In the 1930s, the Paris Opera Ballet, in a state of decline at the time, began to enjoy a renaissance under Serge Lifar. Much admired in France, his choreography was less appreciated abroad. After a further period of stagnation, following the war, this oldest of all ballet companies has now largely regained its former position of eminence in the ballet world, performing an international repertoire. This company boasts one of the strongest ensembles of male dancers anywhere outside Russia.

Restrictions on creative and artistic freedom have limited choreographic development in Soviet Russia and, to a lesser extent in other East European countries. Many new Soviet creations have been full-length works, often based on heroic themes, and expressed in a more or less conventional balletic idiom. Yet, in many respects, the standard of dancing of the best Russian companies, and in particular the classical schooling of the Kirov, remains unequalled.

The Russians are noted for the fluidity and strength of their dancing, and for their powerful elevation. The French are famous for their elegance and technical brilliance. Lyricism as well as subtlety of characterization and style are traditional strong-points of English dancers whilst the Americans are notable for the speed and athleticism of their dancing.

These national characteristics, together with the romantic Bournonville tradition of the Royal Danish Ballet, are the main streams from which flow many tributaries all over the world.

A common denominator in recent years has been the re-emergence, everywhere, of the male ballet dancer, and his new-found pre-eminence.

The Royal Ballet School, in London, and the Ecole de Danse de l'Opéra, in Paris, are generally regarded as the two leading professional ballet schools in Western Europe, with the school of the Royal Danish Ballet, in

Copenhagen, occupying a special place as the guardian of the purest example of authentic nineteenth century style to be found in the professional theatre today.

In the U.S.A., the School of American Ballet is the official school of the New York City Ballet Company, and the other leading American company, American Ballet Theatre, has its own school in New York as well. These two major American ballet companies also draw to a large extent on dancers trained elsewhere, whereas the Paris Opera school and that of the Royal Danish Ballet train mainly nationals of their own countries, specifically for the ranks of their own, respective resident companies. In these European, state subsidized, national institutions, training is entirely free, but selection is very strict and the selection procedure continues throughout the years of training; but when they graduate into the company, the dancers normally have a secure job for the remainder of their dancing lives, and are then pensioned as state employees.

In England, the Royal Ballet School is not a state institution, and tuition is therefore not free. The Lower School is in the Fees Assisted category (parents pay a proportion of the cost, according to their earnings); at the Upper School, British students are normally on Local Authority grants; but no really promising dancer is ever rejected for want of financial means. Auditions are held regularly, both in London and in major regional centres (various arrangements can be made for assessing applicants from abroad). It is usual to audition in the year preceding proposed enrolment. Further information is obtainable from the Auditions' Secretary; the address, together with details of a number of other ballet schools and companies, will be found in the Directory.

The Royal Ballet School exists primarily to train dancers for the two Royal Ballet companies: one is resident at the Royal Opera House, Covent Garden and the other (which is smaller, and takes on the bulk of the Royal Ballet's touring commitments) has a home base at the Sadlers Wells Theatre, in London's Rosebery Avenue.

The Royal Ballet School is divided into two sections. The Lower School, housed at White Lodge in Richmond Park (near London) is a boarding school (day pupils are also accepted) for boys and girls aged eleven to sixteen years, combining professional ballet training with full schooling up to school-leaving age. Pupils then graduate to the Upper School (at Barons

Court, in West London) for a further two to three years of advanced ballet training. Students from other schools, aged sixteen to eighteen, from all over Britain, as well as from other countries, are also accepted into the Upper School. About one third of the students at the Upper School (and a handful at the Lower School) come from abroad, but only a very few foreign dancers can be employed by British companies. This is governed by both union and government regulations.

Besides training dancers for the Royal Ballet companies, the School also helps feed many other companies, notably the London Festival Ballet, Northern Ballet Theatre and the Scottish Ballet as well as sending dancers (both British and foreign) to many companies in Europe and in other countries. (A few do join the Ballet Rambert, but since the late sixties this famous English ballet company has become increasingly modern dance orientated.)

The Lower section of the Royal Ballet School, at White Lodge, is notable for its unusually high proportion of male pupils: over forty boys out of a total of about 120 children. It is remarkable how boys (who, at home, have often been the only male learning ballet in a class of girls) flourish when they find themselves dancing with so many other boys. Pupils are accepted initially on one year's trial; progress and physical development are assessed annually. If, for whatever reason, a pupil is advised to discontinue his ballet training, there is no difficulty, from the educational point of view, in transferring back into an ordinary school. White Lodge is, of course, geared to the needs of classical dancers; sometimes, if it seems appropriate, a boy might eventually be advised to transfer to a stage school, such as the Arts Educational Schools, offering a broader theatrical training and classes in a wider variety of dance styles. A majority of the young men who graduate from White Lodge and then pass successfully through their two to three years at the Upper School are normally employed by one of the Royal Ballet companies. But there can be no guarantee of this and the number of graduates occasionally exceeds the number of places available in the company. However, strong, well-trained dancers like these are always in demand and jobs are fairly easily found, either in other British companies, or abroad.

Further information about career prospects and working conditions will be found in a separate chapter, but perhaps this is the place to point out

Boys working at the Royal Ballet School, White Lodge.

Learning a dance from *The Rake's Progress* in a repertoire class.

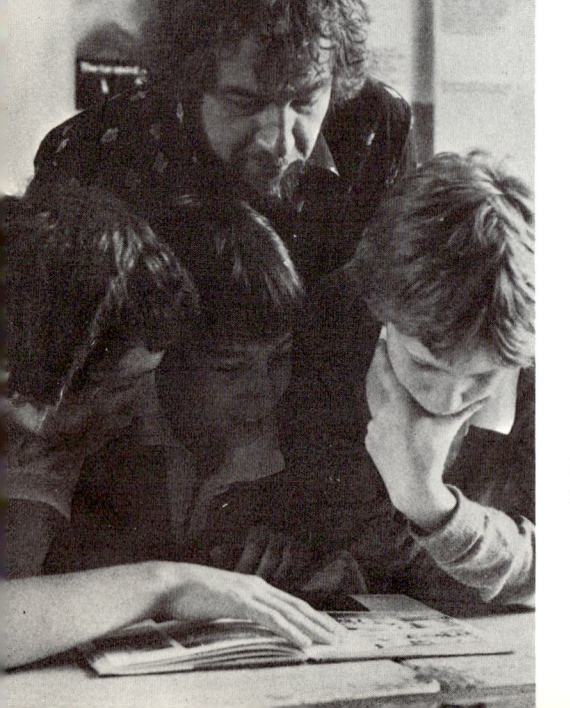

Schoolwork with a member of the academic staff, Peter Davie.

Weight training as a preparation for partnering.

Working in a ballet class.

that, nowadays, most companies like their male dancers to be on the tall side. Five feet eight inches to five feet eleven inches, is roughly the accepted range. Anyone much shorter or much taller than that needs to be exceptionally talented to be employable. Some schools use special medical tests that can predict a child's adult height.

The two leading Soviet Russian schools (and there are several other fine schools in the U.S.S.R.) are the Kirov in Leningrad and the Bolshoi in Moscow. (Prior to the Russian Revolution, in the days of the Imperial Russian Ballet, Leningrad was called St Petersburg and the Kirov was known as the Maryinsky Theatre.) Ballet is immensely popular in Russia, as in most other Soviet bloc countries, and ballet dancers like other artists and sportsmen, occupy something of a privileged position in Soviet society. Their training and education is financed entirely by the state, and those who do well are assured of secure employment. The dancers are generally very well trained (although, of course, little is known about the failure rate in such a closed society), but the lack of artistic freedom undoubtedly imposes severe limitations on all concerned. However, this book is concerned mainly with dancing as a career for men in Western Europe and America, and in other countries reflecting the balletic traditions of the West. Canada, Australia, South Africa and New Zealand all have flourishing ballet schools and companies in the British tradition, and the standard of teaching is often exceptionally high.

In Europe, in the established nineteenth century tradition, most major cities maintain their own ballet groups, mainly to dance in opera productions; but, increasingly, a set number of performances each month is reserved for programmes of ballet. Local arrangements vary, as do standards, and there is a considerable amount of moving of dancers and ballet masters between companies, from one season to another. Stuttgart and Antwerp are at present among the most established centres, Nederlands Danstheater leads the field in the fusion of classical and modern dance techniques, and Maurice Béjart, with his Ballet du XXème Siècle, in Brussels, is famous for his unique brand of heroic dance spectacle, immensely popular with young audiences, and particularly notable for the outstanding talent of many of his male dancers. Most of these companies employ dancers of various nationalities, including many from Britain and the U.S.A.

Apart from the two major American ballet companies already mentioned, there are many other flourishing groups in the U.S.A., where the standard of ballet in general, and that of male dancing in particular, has risen dramatically in recent years. Robert Joffrey and Gerald Arpino, as well as Eliot Feld are among the distinguished American choreographers who have headed their own companies, and Arthur Mitchell has broken new ground with his all-black, classically-based Dance Theatre of Harlem. There are several other fine professional ballet companies, notably in Pennsylvania, San Francisco, Boston and Washington. Many of the most talented young men discovered and trained by the schools serving these companies gain scholarships to the School of American Ballet and the American Ballet Theatre School and are subsequently employed by the major, New York based companies.

The Civic Ballets are a whole network of amateur and semi-professional ballet groups, stretching from coast to coast, and drawing their dancers from local ballet schools in particular regions. They play an important role both in promoting ballet in the U.S.A. and as a testing-ground for up and coming young performers and choreographers.

All dancers have to keep in daily training throughout their careers, and this is particularly vital for ballet dancers. The demands made on the human body by the conventions of the classical technique require constant practice under an experienced teacher. The distribution and placing of body weight, the alignment of hips and limbs, the correct use of 'turn-out', the carriage and co-ordination of arms and head, the precise use and control of the feet and the back; all these things require continual, minute adjustments of detail in order for the dancer to be able to maintain his technical proficiency. In this respect, for the duration of his active career, even the most experienced professional dancer continues to work under the guidance of a teacher.

For students and professionals alike, the daily ballet class lasts an average of one and a half hours (companies with heavy rehearsal schedules often have a slightly shorter class, as do very young students). The basic format of the class is always very much the same. First come the exercises at the barre, to warm up all the muscles slowly and systematically and generally prepare the whole body for dancing, with specific concentration on the action of the legs and feet, the control of the back and the placement of the hips. Next come the exercises in the centre of the studio. Basically these are

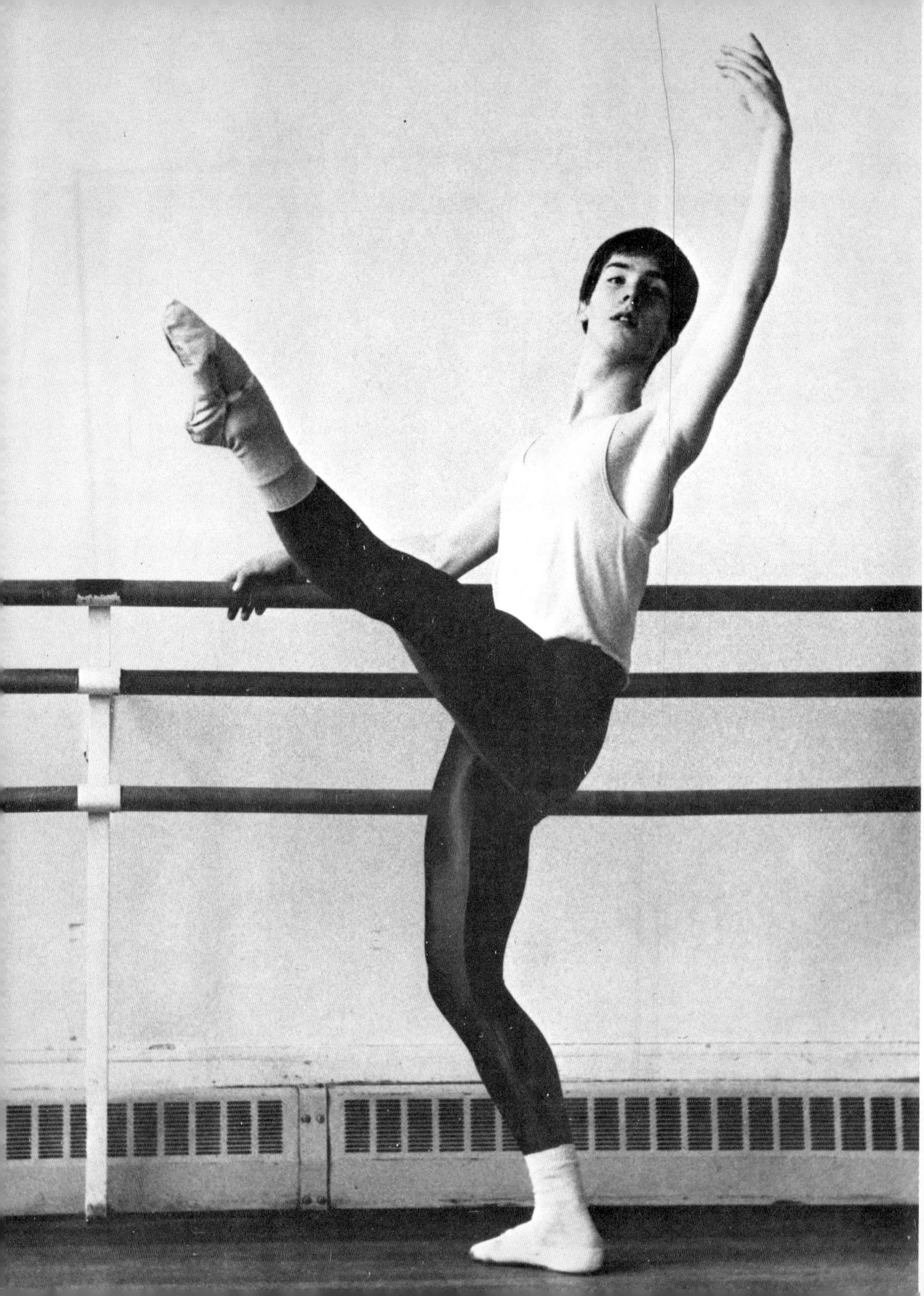

Four pictures of Philip Broomhead, a graduate student at the Royal Ballet School.

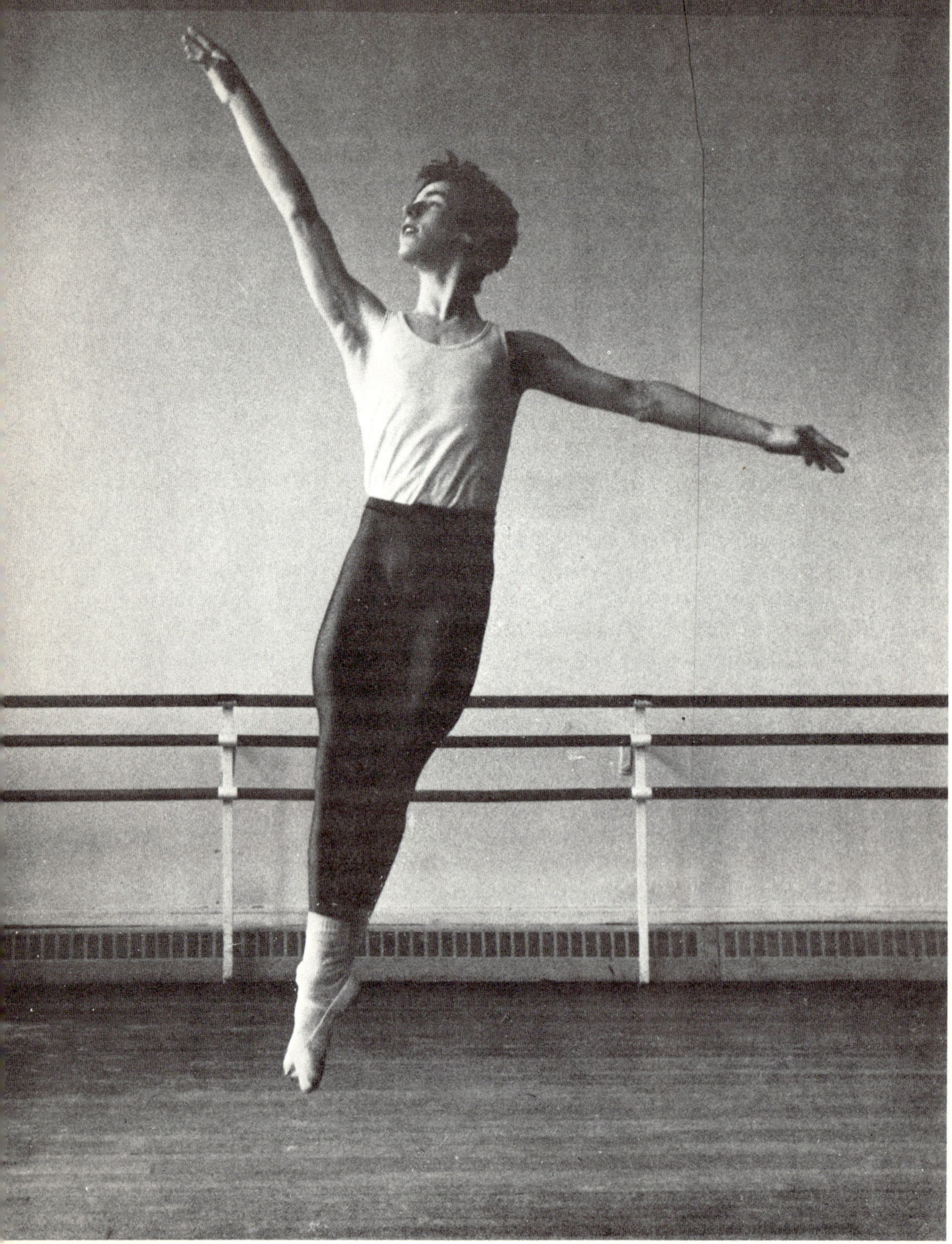

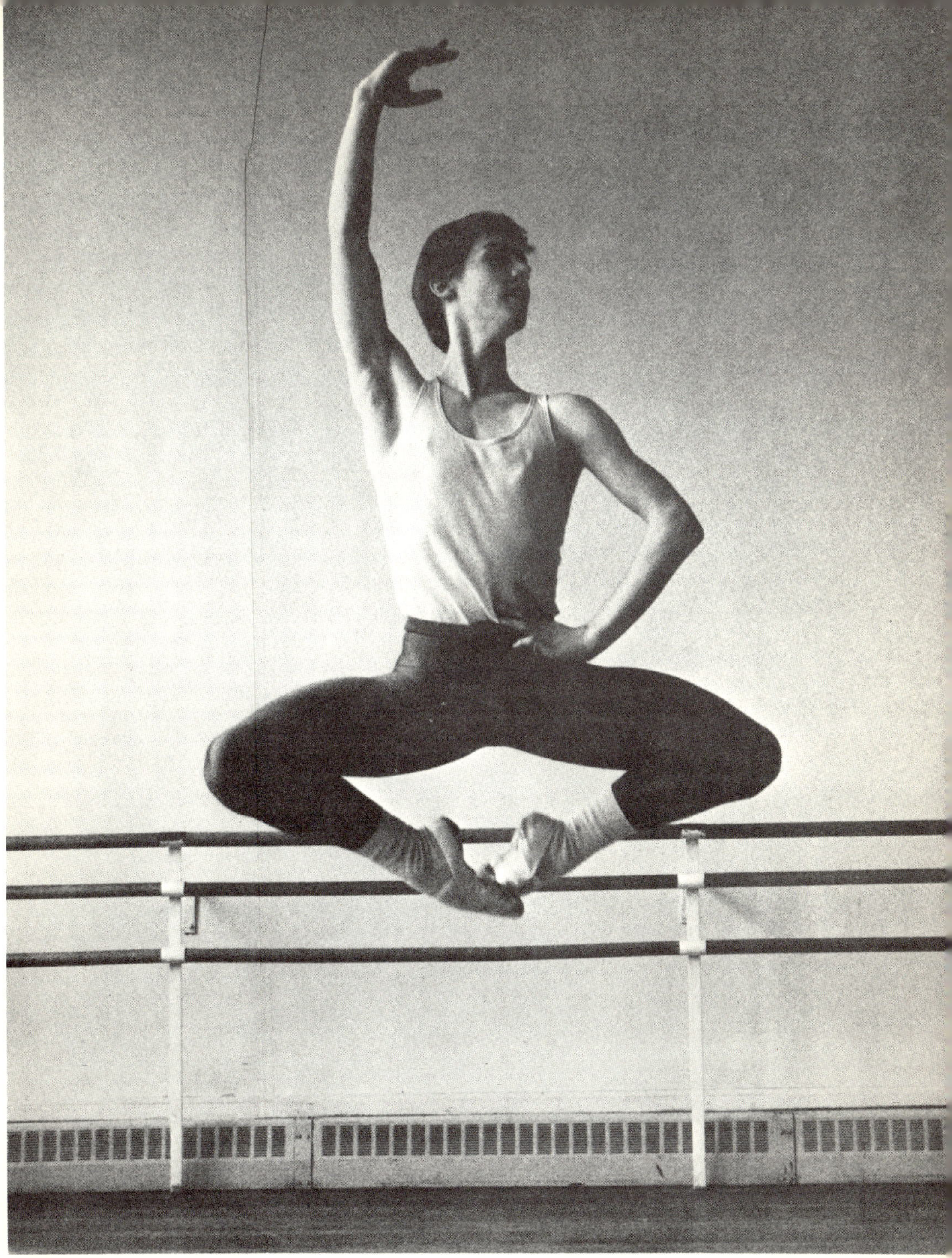

a repetition and an elaboration of the barre work, but now performed without its support, and with the introduction of many changes of direction and an increased use of the arms and head. Next come those sections of the lesson concentrating on *adage* (slow, sustained movements which develop the dancers' sense of balance and feeling for 'line') and the many and varied turning and spinning movements referred to as *tours* and *pirouettes*. Male ballet dancers are required to excel at these, as they are at steps of 'elevation'. The latter conclude the class and consist of all the different types of jumping movements, first small and simple, then becoming gradually more complex (including movements of *batterie*, in which the dancer's feet interweave in the air, and the legs are beaten one against the other whilst he is jumping) getting higher and bigger and finally travelling, beating and turning in all directions. This is the section of the class boys usually enjoy most.

In addition to his daily classical class, a senior professional student's weekly timetable will normally include several sessions devoted to coaching specific areas of his technique, as well as classes in *pas de deux* (often called 'double work', this is the study of partnering and is discussed fully in a separate chapter). Traditionally, ballet dancers also study some form of character or national dancing; many ballets include dances in the Hungarian, Polish, Spanish or other styles, as well as classical mime (the latter is becoming increasingly obsolete). Modern or contemporary dance classes, once taboo for classical dancers, are now increasingly found on the curriculum of ballet schools. In the final years of training, repertoire classes assume increasing importance — here the student learns excerpts from the classics and from ballets currently in the parent company's repertoire.

The special circumstances affecting late beginners are discussed elsewhere but, ideally, an aspiring classical ballet dancer will join a professional school between the ages of ten and twelve and spend six to nine years in full-time training. In these days of 'instant art', the slow, methodical, meticulous and highly selective and competitive training of a classical ballet dancer may seem almost something of an anachronism. But, like the study of classical music, the beauty, harmony and controlled strength of classical dance admit of no shortcuts.

Male students of the National Ballet School of Canada in *Here We Come* choreographed by Erik Bruhn. (*Photograph by Jeanette Edessi Collins*)

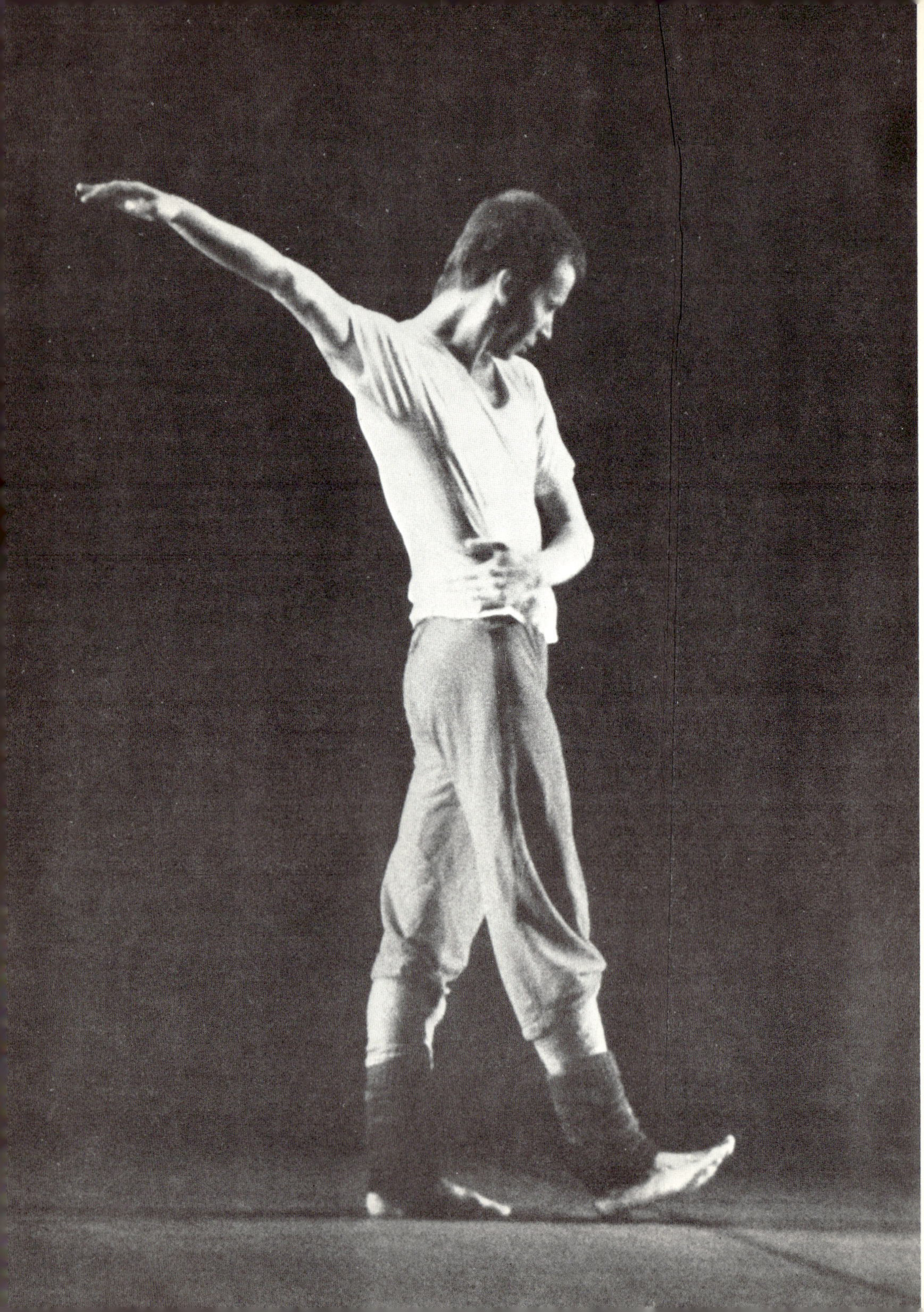

4

MODERN OR CONTEMPORARY DANCE

From the first years of the twentieth century, there was in the U.S.A. and in central Europe (separately, but simultaneously) a movement away from the academic structure of classical ballet towards a freer, more natural, more expressive way of dancing. This developed along several different paths and in many different ways.

There was no set vocabulary of movements or steps. Shoes and physically restricting costumes were discarded, and so was virtuosity. Various forms evolved and some of the names used to describe them included 'free dance', 'new dance', 'barefoot dance' and 'expressionist dance'.

These new approaches varied from the 'free dance' of Isadora Duncan and the ethnic mysticism and music visualization of Ruth St Denis and Ted Shawn in the U.S.A., to Rudolph von Laban's scientific analysis of movement and the expressive drama of Kurt Joos and Mary Wigman's dancing in Central Europe. But all were united in their fierce opposition to what they saw as the superficiality and artificiality of classical ballet, and in their passionate desire to create new ways of dancing. The result is what came to be known as modern dance.

This is not a very precise term, but a useful (and necessary) means of describing a way of dancing which was totally different from ballet. I use the past tense quite deliberately because, over the years, ballet and modern dance have both changed and evolved a great deal. In spite of important

Tom Jobe of the London Contemporary Dance Theatre
in rehearsal for Richard Alston's *Rainbow Bandit*.

Patrick Harding-Irmer of the London Contemporary Dance Theatre in Robert Cohan's *Class*. This work illustrates various aspects of the contemporary dance vocabulary.

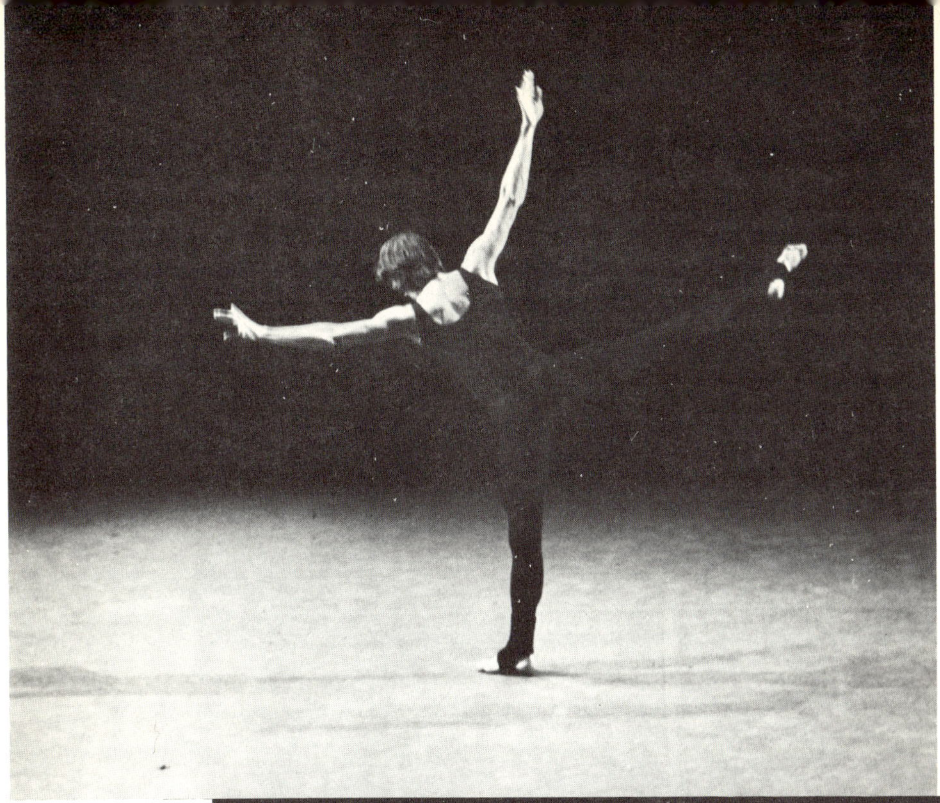

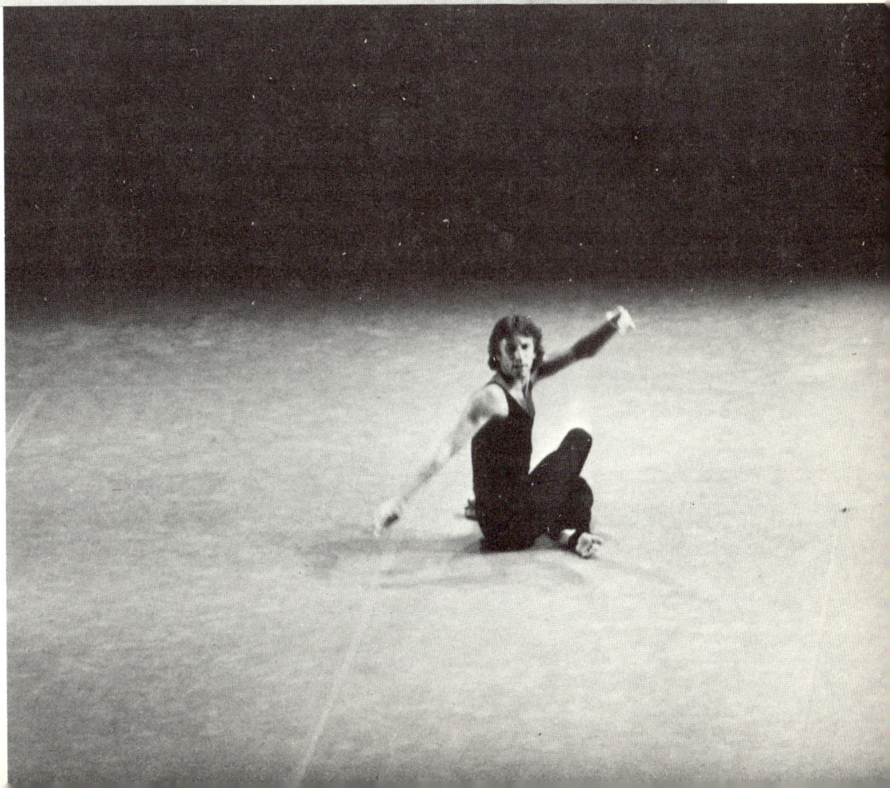

differences, these two forms of dance are now no longer as diametrically opposed to one another as was once the case; many professional dancers now do both.

Strictly speaking, the word 'contemporary' means 'belonging to the same time'. Current popular usage extends this to mean 'of the present day'. In this sense, the expression 'contemporary dance' ought to include ballet in its present-day forms, many of which are as different from those of the early years of the century as present-day modern dance is from that of the 1920s.

Be that as it may, the expression 'contemporary dance' has now, in fact, come to mean the non-balletic, serious dance of today, and the leading British modern dance company is indeed called the London Contemporary Dance Theatre, and its school the London School of Contemporary Dance.

This school, which is recognized by the Department of Education and Science as a College of Further Education, is unique in that it is a full-time professional school, linked to a full-time professional company. In most other cases where a modern dance performing group is based on a school, it is a privately-run studio school. Elsewhere, contemporary dance is taught in colleges or in the dance departments of schools such as the famous Juilliard School of Music in New York. Such courses may be linked to performing groups, but normally not on a professional basis. Of course, not all students studying at the London School of Contemporary Dance are there with a view to joining the London Contemporary Dance Theatre.

There are about 150 full-time students at the school, with 300 children, teenagers and adults taking regular or part-time classes, and a similar number attending short vacation courses. The dance training is based on contemporary American dance techniques, mainly the technique of Martha Graham, but tries to give as broad a base as possible. (This also includes classes in ballet technique, folk dance and historical dance.)

Martha Graham remains one of the most influential figures in modern dance. Whereas the work of a number of her predecessors, using the simplest of dance vocabularies, depended largely on the force of their own personalities and was unable to survive its creators, Graham evolved a movement technique which could be handed on to a new generation. Robert Cohan, a pupil of Graham's and for many years her dance partner, helped to found the London School of Contemporary Dance on her principles.

Modern or Contemporary Dance

The best dancers from this school are able to graduate into the London Contemporary Dance Theatre. Robert Cohan is this Company's director and its principal choreographer. But although, in many fundamental ways, he continues the Graham tradition, Cohan does much to encourage other ideas and to stimulate new developments. The teaching of some of the faculty at the London School of Contemporary Dance reflects the influence of other leading modern dance styles, and short courses are given from time to time by visiting teachers specializing in other techniques, such as that of José Limon.

Even more important than this is the encouragement of indigenous creative talent. The school is highly geared to the teaching of dance composition and the encouragement of young choreographers.

Based on a full-time school, and offering year-round employment to nearly twenty dancers (about half of them men) London Contemporary Dance Theatre occupies a unique place in the modern dance world.

Yet, to some people, this very stability seems suspect — they regard London Contemporary Dance Theatre almost as part of the 'establishment'. This is one of the reasons why numerous small groups exist and continue to spring up both in and out of London. Some are based on the choreographic ideas and personal philosophy of one particular dancer/choreographer, others lean towards forms of joint creativity.

Unfettered by Graham traditions, or those of any other established style, there is a sense in which some of these people could be said to be the true standard-bearers of contemporary dance. Many certainly see themselves as such. Small, experimental groups have always been the lifeblood of modern dance, giving new impetus to old ideas and boldly exploring uncharted territory. Perhaps they are more necessary than ever, now that the mainstream of contemporary dance, particularly in England, is going through a period of consolidating ground and putting down roots. Yet, although there is much integrity and some genuine creativity, there are also elements of pseudo-intellectualism and half-baked philosophy, as well as much striking of political attitudes, to be found in the more radical of the fringe groups.

To the newcomer on the contemporary dance scene, my advice would be to begin by concentrating on acquiring a sound technical training, as broadly based as possible, and to keep an open mind about the philosophy

Dancers of the
London Contemporary Dance Theatre
in Robert Cohan's *Class*.

Modern or Contemporary Dance

Dancers of the London Contemporary Dance Theatre
rehearsing for Richard Alston's
Rainbow Bandit
on the stage of the Sadler's Wells Theatre.

and politics of the fringe. An aspiring professional dancer's first job is to learn to control and understand his own body, and that needs a clear, receptive mind as much as anything else.

One of the advantages of modern dance is that it is possible to start serious training considerably later than would normally be acceptable in classical ballet. Provided you have a suitable physique (a flexible spine, mobile joints, strong legs and a strong back) and the necessary athletic co-ordination, it is possible to start training in your late teens, or even early twenties, and still become a good modern dancer. The different physical demands of much contemporary dance generally also make it possible to enjoy a longer active career than is usual in classical ballet. A much wider range of height and physical type is accepted and encouraged in the modern dance field than in the ballet world.

The degree of complexity of classical ballet technique requires many years of concentration on the acquisition of purely technical skills, but modern dance is much more concerned with the exploration of movement. Yet, although contemporary dance is essentially a form of physical expression in which there are no academic rules to hold you back, the standard of technical proficiency demanded by many present-day choreographers is so high that it is necessary for the dancer to submit to a rigorous, formalized physical training. But whereas the essence of ballet lies in the exploration of its formal structure, the modern dancer must be prepared to abandon formal structure in order to explore movement in its widest sense.

Present-day trends tend to concentrate on shifting the emphasis from the dramatic content of movement to its motor action. There is much careful study of how movements are articulated and of how the weight of the body is shifted. The movements are made to emanate outwards from the centre of the body or the spine, and the dancers learn to explore the use of focus and dynamics. Whereas classical ballet seeks to eliminate visible physical effort, modern dance often makes positive use of it. Other major differences from ballet technique are to be found in the extremely flexible use of the spine and in the strong use of the floor. Modern dancers work barefoot, thus increasing their sense of being firmly rooted in the floor, rather than being poised, ready for flight. Jumps do form an increasingly important part of contemporary dance techniques, but their character is generally less ethereal and bouncy than balletic steps of elevation. Controlled falls and rolls are an essential and characteristic ingredient of modern dance training. Like all dancers, modern dancers need strong, flexible feet but the shape and line of the foot is of less consequence than in ballet; the use of turn-out is demanded in some contemporary dance styles much more than in others, but is not as fundamental to the whole technique as it is with classical ballet.

The whole area of double-work (lifts, partnering and other forms of physical support) is generally more limited than in ballet, and such skills as the modern dancer does require are usually acquired in ballet double-work classes or in the course of choreographic rehearsals. Contact-improvisation — the physical contact of two people, each using their own body-weight against that of their partner to initiate spontaneous movement patterns in space — is an area recently much explored by contemporary dancers such as Steve Paxton.

Not all modern dance companies, either in Europe or in the U.S.A., are able to keep their dancers in full-time regular employment all year round. One particularly notable exception is the London Contemporary Dance Theatre. Probably the only other contemporary style company to perform even more frequently is the Alvin Ailey Company (in the U.S.A.). Many groups pay their dancers for limited seasons, or even per performance. Their income generally has to be supplemented, often by teaching; some time is also taken up with residencies at colleges and in universities — indeed, in the U.S.A. in particular, modern dance plays a big role in campus life. This is becoming increasingly true in other countries too.

In spite of the relative precariousness of their existence, the best American modern dance groups have been responsible for some of the most exciting work to be seen in the theatre in the past few decades. Among the most influential have been Merce Cunningham (originally from the Martha Graham Company) and Paul Taylor (who studied at Juilliard and with Graham). Both formed their own companies, developing highly individual styles, as did José Limon, whose mentor was Doris Humphrey. (She and her associate, Charles Weidman, were two of the great pioneers of American modern dance.)

There are many basic similarities in the techniques of these main schools, but there are also important differences, particularly in areas such as the use of the arms and in the approach to timing and phrasing. It is perfectly possible for the well-trained dancer to adjust to these differences, but this is something that requires work and concentrated thought. It is important to understand that these variations sometimes stem from fundamental differences between one contemporary dance group and another concerning the nature and purpose of dance itself, and the function of choreography.

Whereas the aim of the earliest pioneers of modern dance had been to develop a way of moving that could expressively portray the emotions and concerns of twentieth century women and men, half-way through this century new trends began to emerge. Some dancers and choreographers now took the view that using dance as a means of dramatic expression was placing unnecessary limitations on the choreographer's capacity for inventing and using movement. They began to think of dance in a much more abstract way, using movement rather as a non-figurative painter uses colour, texture and line.

The entire concept of the relationship of music to dance was revolutionized by pioneers like Merce Cunningham; in collaboration with the avant-garde composer John Cage, he arranged his choreography totally independently from the accompanying sound. This a-synchronic use of dance and music can be seen as a reflection of the way many present-day activities take place against a background of unrelated sound. He also changed traditional ideas concerning the structure of a dance, allowing chance devices to determine in what order the movements were to be performed; this could be different at each performance.

Whereas early modern dance had continued to use the stage space in the traditional theatrical way, focussing attention on central figures to maximum dramatic effect, Cunningham was one of the first to experiment with making the audience see the stage action in new and different ways. In a further attempt to alter our way of looking at dance, performances were given in art galleries, in gymnasiums, out of doors — anywhere where the dancers could show their work to an audience. The spectators were seated in the round or might even come and go during the performance, depending on the locality and the circumstances. All this added new dimensions to the way people thought of and looked at dance. These were dance 'events' rather than performances in the conventional sense of the word.

Artists like Alwin Nikolais sought to depersonalize dance completely by using the dancers as only one of many elements in an audio-visual, total theatre concept, with props devised to extend the dancers' physical size in space. He broke away from the psychological and introspective dance dramas of some of the moderns, seeing man as part of an ecological and environmental universe, free from overtones of psychology, religious mysticism or hero-identification.

Whilst some dance creators experimented with ideas of minimal movement or of audience alienation, others deliberately used non-dancers in experiments intended to focus attention on everyday movements taken out of their normal context.

Reflecting similar contemporary experiments in the social field, some groups adopted systems of collective decision-making, with all the participants involved in creating the choreography of a new piece, often using improvisation as a basis for their work.

Other groups — particularly of black Americans — found fresh inspiration in ancient ethnic dance roots.

The richness and diversity of the creative work done in the field of American contemporary dance in the past few decades are astounding. It is impossible within the scope of this book to give full credit to the many creative individuals and groups involved, but two of the most original and talented to emerge in the 1970s were Twyla Tharp, with her exquisite, often humorous understanding of style and rhythm, and the Pilobolus Dance Theatre who have totally succeeded in their collaborative approach to dance creation with works of astonishing originality, vitality and skill. Without resorting to Alwin Nikolais' complex use of theatrical tricks and gadgetry, Pilobolus seems to have carried his vision of the universe a stage further.

Although little that is as original and influential as the very best American experimental dance has yet emerged in Britain (or anywhere else for that matter) there are many active and adventurous creative artists at work.

The creative backbone of London Contemporary Dance Theatre has been provided by choreographers like Robert Cohan, Robert North, Micha Bergese and Siobhan Davies, whilst the many active contemporary dance choreographers working in Britain in the late seventies included: Richard Alston, Christopher Bruce, Ian Spink, Rosemary Butcher, Janet Smith, Tamara McLorg and Ross McKim. Much experimental work has been done by a number of other choreographers associated with the X6 Dance

Collective.

Several ballet-based companies, such as the Ballet Rambert in England, the Robert Joffrey Company in the U.S.A. and the Nederlands Danstheater in Holland, include in their repertoires a number of works by leading contemporary dance choreographers (among them Tetley, Taylor, Sokolow, Tharp, Limon, Falco, Bruce, Morrice and Butler) and therefore require their dancers to be proficient in both ballet and modern dance techniques, a trend which is now spreading more and more throughout the dance world.

Modern dance is acquiring an increasing following in Canada and Australia as well as in traditionalist countries like France, where Carolyn Carlson has succeeded in establishing an experimental group within the conservative confines of the Paris Opera.

MAAS Movers is the name of Britain's leading black dance company. Other recent additions to the modern dance scene in Britain include two very small but remarkably active groups, the EMMA Dance Company, operating from Loughborough in the Midlands and the Extemporary Dance Company, which is London-based. And there are several other groups, some of them operating only intermittently.

So there are many opportunities for good male dancers in the contemporary dance field. For the young man with the necessary talent, skill and staying-power, it can offer an intellectually-stimulating and rewarding way of life, with more opportunities for creative work, and perhaps a greater sense of personal contribution than would normally be the case in either ballet or showbusiness.

Robert North and the masked figure of Tom Jobe, of the London Contemporary Dance Theatre in Robert Cohan's *Masque of Separation.*

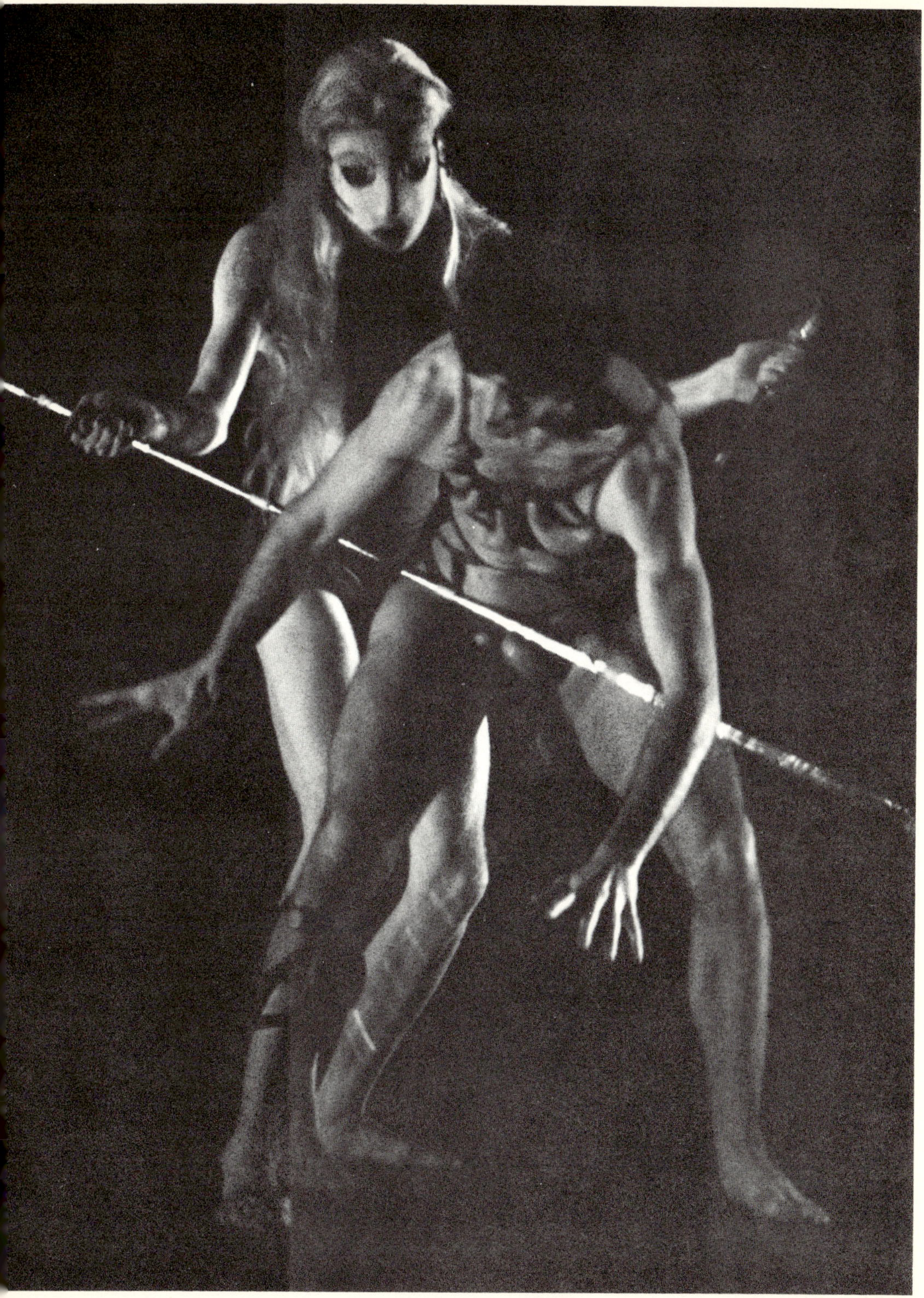

Charles Augins, star of the London production of *Bubblin' Brown Sugar*.

5

SHOWBUSINESS

At its worst, a career in showbusiness can be very precarious indeed and too many young (and not so young) hopefuls find they spend more time 'resting' (the theatrical euphemism for being out of work) than performing. Working conditions can be tawdry and uncomfortable and the work itself often boringly repetitive. But at its best, for the lucky few who make it to the top, there can be rich financial rewards and the excitement of working with some of the most talented directors and choreographers in the world. The skill, precision, imagination and sheer professionalism to be found at the top of the showbusiness world are second to none and, provided one is realistic about the necessity of looking eventually to a second career (be it in teaching, directing, choreography, acting or — more often than not — in a completely different field) the satisfaction of even a short-lived career in showbusiness is usually well worth the inevitable gamble involved.

Nowadays a showbusiness dancer must also be able to sing and act. He can either study at a stage school where, combined with general secondary education, he will be taught singing and acting as well as various types of dance; or he can attend classes at a dance studio and study privately with a vocal and a drama coach.

From the age of eight or nine years, tap lessons will provide the young dancer with invaluable training in rhythmic skill and co-ordination. It is advisable not to start jazz dance classes until the student is in his teens. Apart from the fact that there is implicit in much jazz dance a sexuality which is beyond the understanding of a young child, some of the exercises used in jazz classes can be too strenuous for a young boy's body. Far better to start off with a few simple ballet lessons: this is the best way for the beginner — be he a child or a teenager — to acquire the fundamental body-placement which will give him a sound basis for all his future training.

In Britain, the Imperial Society of Teachers of Dancing also has an excellent syllabus, especially designed for boys, of what is called Modern Stage Dance (not to be confused with Martha Graham-type modern dance). This is carefully graded to prepare youngsters gradually for musical comedy and jazz work.

Depending on the fashion of the day, showbusiness choreography (be it for stage shows, films, television, revues or nightclubs) can include specialized forms of movement such as tap, jazz, ballet, acrobatics, and various types of national or ethnic dance, as well as all types of social or ballroom dancing. The latter includes anything from the waltz, the Charleston or the tango, via rock 'n roll, to disco dancing — which is really an up-dated, more physical form of ballroom dancing. Fashions in dance come and go rapidly, and showbusiness dancing always reflects these changes. The early 1970s, for instance, saw a big revival of tap dancing which, by the end of the decade, had been superseded by disco. Although all these specialized forms retain their own identity and (according to popular demand) continue to be taught by specialist teachers, many of their characteristic elements have gradually become absorbed into the general body of what is loosely termed jazz dance.

Europe and the rest of the world look to the U.S.A. for the lead in most forms of showbusiness and, in the American entertainment world, jazz dance now dominates the scene.

There are probably almost as many slightly different styles of jazz dance as there are teachers and choreographers working in showbusiness: it is an ever-changing dance form, continually absorbing new influences. In fact, the term jazz dance (particularly in the U.S.A.) is now used to encompass such a wide range of styles that it has virtually replaced the old expression 'musical comedy dancing' as a means of describing showbusiness dancing.

Unlike ballet, jazz dance has no set vocabulary of steps. Like jazz music, it is continually evolving and has come a long way from the spontaneity of its original American negro roots.

Today, a typical jazz dance class starts with warm-up exercises, followed by floor exercises (stretching). Next come the isolation exercises, in which the dancer learns to perform isolated movements with the head, neck and shoulders, arms, torso, pelvis and hips. These are generally followed by turns and jumping movements and then progressions — series of kicks, runs, etc., moving across the floor. The final section of the lesson is devoted to learning a jazz combination (often quite long and complicated) choreographed by the teacher. Sometimes a new combination, in a different style, is arranged to round off every lesson; sometimes a class will continue to work on the same combination for several lessons, perfecting details of technique and style.

This logical, systematic approach to the teaching of a jazz dance technique is exemplified in the work of the famous New York-based jazz teacher, Luigi. Most teachers schooled in his method will have a serious approach to the teaching of jazz. Other leading teachers include Ron Forella in New York and Matt Mattox, an American who has taught extensively both in London and in Paris.

With many different teachers working in many different styles, it can be difficult to know where to begin. To the young man starting jazz classes, I would offer the following advice. When selecting a jazz teacher, don't necessarily opt for the most popular one. Popular classes, with thirty or forty students on the floor, are not the best place to start. Go to a smaller school, to a teacher who is going to give you personal attention and take the trouble to teach you a good basic jazz technique (if possible, in the Luigi tradition). Also be sure to attend some good, basic ballet classes. Once you have been schooled in the basics of jazz technique and have learnt to discipline and control your movements, you can easily move on to learn a wide variety of jazz styles from all the most popular current exponents.

It can be very useful to have a little training in basic gymnastics or acrobatics. All specialities can, from time to time, earn you extra money in a particular show. Apparatus work is not necessary, but the ability to do cartwheels, handstands, walk-overs, etc., is always an asset. However, there is no need for dancers to have a great deal of acrobatic training: if the director needs specialist acrobatics in his show he will hire acrobats. Learning to lift and partner a girl is another important skill, and this is best learnt in a ballet double-work class.

The physical and technical requirements for a jazz dancer are not as stringent as those for a classical ballet dancer. Provided he has the necessary

Senior pupils of
the Arts Educational School
in London in a jazz class.

William Walker, a student of the Arts Educational School in London, in a tap dancing class.

natural talent and physical facility, it is possible for a jazz dancer to start training in his late teens or early twenties. He can get by with a little less turn-out, extension and strength than a classical dancer (although he, too, needs strong, flexible feet). He should be well co-ordinated and needs to have an excellent sense of rhythm but, above all, he must have a natural flair for the jazz idiom. This is an indefinable quality, something I can only describe as a real feeling for jazz, a feeling which generates a natural and spontaneous movement response to jazz music.

In showbusiness much depends on current trends, and on the individual style and preference of each choreographer; so it is difficult to generalize about things like the ideal height for a jazz dancer. Some choreographers do like using shorter people, and there are shows which specifically require a variety of physical types in the cast; but on the whole, and especially for night-club work, tall dancers are very much in demand. The men in Las Vegas-type shows are usually five feet ten inches to six feet tall.

No matter how talented and well trained he is, a dancer cannot get straight into a show on Broadway or in London's West End. For that he has to be a full Equity member. Equity is the trades union to which most professional dancers in Britain belong. In the U.S.A. membership is divided between several different unions, including Equity, A.F.T.R.A., A.G.M.A., A.G.V.A. and S.A.G.

In Britain a dancer must work a total of forty-four weeks to earn full Equity status. This is achieved by doing out-of-town shows such as seaside revues and Christmas pantomimes in the smaller provincial theatres or by working abroad on an Equity contract. In the U.S.A. a young dancer starting out should aim to get into a good, residential Summer Stock company. (These are local theatre groups presenting revivals of popular musical shows in summer repertory seasons.) Starting at fifteen or sixteen years of age, he could do this for two or three summers. Further information would be obtained by writing to the Municipal Opera in a city like St Louis, Pittsburg or Kansas City. Auditions are sometimes held locally and sometimes take place in a big centre like Chicago. Working a couple of seasons in Summer Stock, a young dancer could get a dozen Broadway revivals under his belt before trying for the big time. Working in one of the better Summer Stock companies will also give the beginner the experience of appearing alongside good guest stars, as well as the opportunity of working with new, young choreographers; some may prove to be valuable future contacts.

Certain groups also do Winter Stock, and young people can sometimes get an opportunity of playing more important roles in the cut-versions of Broadway Shows presented by the so-called Dinner Theatres.

Opportunities on this sort of scale do not, as yet, exist in Britain; but a variety of work is available and auditions are advertised in trade newspapers like *The Stage and Television Today* (published in London every Thursday). The principal equivalent in the U.S.A. is *Backstage*. Advertisements will usually specify whether the audition is for Equity members only, or whether it is an open call. A dancer who does not yet have a union card should go along to an open call; if he's really good, he might possibly get into a big show in this way.

But auditions are not always advertised. This is particularly true of work on television and in films. Dancers often hear about auditions by word-of-mouth, at class, in one of the big, popular studios. In an over-crowded profession, where plum jobs are hard to come by, news of auditions is often a closely guarded secret; but the newcomer soon learns to keep his ear to the ground. It usually pays to keep on good terms with so-called 'working dancers', those employed regularly by a well-known choreographer; many choreographers, particularly in television, tend to use the same little clique of dancers again and again. This is also true of the film world — it's very hard to break into, but for the lucky few it can provide lucrative and comparatively regular employment.

It is usually easier to get into the nightclub end of showbusiness. In the U.S.A., in particular, the financial rewards for nightclub work can be very tempting and many dancers find that working somewhere like Las Vegas is a good way of saving money to help them go to the big cities and study seriously with the best teachers and eventually get into top Broadway shows and Hollywood films. Unfortunately, British dancers are not normally allowed to work in the U.S.A. (and vice versa); well-paid nightclub and show work is sometimes available in other countries (and on some big cruise ships), but dancers taking up such jobs should always make sure they get a Standard Equity Overseas Contract.

In Britain the Equity *minimum* wage (at the time of writing) is £50 a week; but for a big London West End show, a dancer in the chorus can

Dancers in the London production of *Bubblin' Brown Sugar*.

Mark Calderon of the Olga Fricker School in Los Angeles, jumping in a jazz class.

expect to earn up to £100 for eight shows a week. On Broadway he could earn as much as $500 a week. Contracts can be for a specified, limited period, or else for the run of the show. If it turns out to be a big success that could mean being stuck in the same show for a very long time!

In a regular show the dancers get a paid vacation; but they can usually opt to work through this for double pay. The Dance Captain (or Line Captain) is a senior dancer in the show who is also responsible for supervising rehearsals and his additional duties can earn him quite a bit of extra money. He can sometimes help hire new dancers and may later get to re-stage a show in which he once worked.

As principal dance roles are very few and far between in musical shows nowadays, dancers seeking promotion out of the chorus line need to start specializing seriously as actor-dancers or singer-dancers (as opposed to dancers who sing and act a little).

Whilst waiting for an opportunity of a solo role in a new stage show, film or television special, good acting experience — and good money — can be obtained by making television or film commercials; at this point it becomes essential to secure the services of a good theatrical agent.

Ideally, the dancer will already be appearing in a show and can therefore get a prospective agent to come along and see him performing. If this is not possible, it will be necessary for the dancer to show the agent a résumé of his previous experience and a portfolio of photographs of himself. If the agent agrees to take him on as a client, he will have to sign a contract agreeing to pay him a commission on any work the agent gets him. Finding the right agent is important and the newcomer should seek the advice of experienced colleagues.

The same applies to securing the services of a good tax consultant who can advise the dancer on the wide variety of expenses that can usually be claimed in connection with theatre work.

Showbusiness also offers a number of professional opportunities for child performers. The employment of children and juveniles is strictly controlled by law. Licences have to be obtained by the producer or director of the show. Regulations vary, but the Greater London Council, for instance, does not normally allow children under the age of twelve to perform on more than two days a week, and the total number of shows a year must not exceed forty-six. On tour, a tutor must be provided to assure the child's schooling for a specified number of hours each day.

A group of dancers in a television production called *Must Wear Tights*. Choreography by Dougie Squires. (*Photograph by courtesy of Thames Television*)

Margaret Barbieri and Desmond Kelly of the Sadler's Wells Royal Ballet in the *pas de deux* from *The Two Pigeons* by Ashton. This is the epitome of the love duet in Dancing.

6

THE PARTNER

All movements where one dancer is supported or partnered by another are covered by the term 'double-work'. This can vary from the 'supported *adage*' of classical ballet, with the male, referred to balletically as the 'cavalier' (a term implying gentlemanly attendance upon a lady) partnering the woman in a formal, stylized manner, to the quasi-acrobatic lifts and other manipulations of two or more bodies much used by present-day choreographers.

Nowadays the demands made in this area by most choreographers (particularly in the field of ballet) are so advanced, that young men in the *corps de ballet* frequently find themselves having to perform feats of partnering previously expected only of principal dancers.

The art of partnering is now very much an integral and essential part of every male dancer's professional expertise. This is particularly true of the male ballet dancer; but an ability to partner, to some degree, is also a necessity in most other forms of theatre dance — as it is, of course, in many areas of social dancing.

The acrobatic elements, as well as the overt sexuality characteristic of much present-day double-work are a comparatively recent development in the context of serious theatre dance (although, of course, they have long been used in the world of cabaret entertainment).

The essence of the balletic *pas de deux*, on the other hand, is already to be found in the mediaeval *danse à deux*, with its connotations of chivalry and gallantry.

The male–female element, the dance of one man with one woman, the display of formalized courtship — these were at the heart of that great tradition of social dancing which flourished at the courts of the European monarchs; as we have seen, this was one of the roots from which classical ballet was to grow.

With the development of *pointe* work, early in the nineteenth century, the female ballet dancer acquired an aerial, ethereal quality. This impression of flight was further increased by having the male lift and carry the woman. Indeed, in a ballet like the second act of *Giselle*, where the ballerina is playing the role of a spirit, risen from the grave and flying, gossamer-like, through the air, the impression given in the passages of double-work should be not so much that of the man *lifting* the woman, as of Albrecht — a live human being — drawing the floating spirit of the dead Giselle back to earth (a subtlety of style all too often ignored in present-day renderings). The man's ability to lift his partner and yet give the impression that, in reality, it is she who is flying away from him, requires great skill and strength on his part, as well as perfect co-ordination between the separate actions done by each of the two dancers in all preparatory movements. The correct use of the rhythmic impulse of the music can be of immense advantage in achieving this mutual co-ordination.

When she is dancing *sur les pointes*, on the tips of her toes, the base on which the female dancer is standing is reduced to an absolute minimum, giving her very limited control over her movements. For any very sustained movement she needs the assistance of a partner to help her find and maintain her point of balance.

The concept of line, by which we mean the geometrical shapes made in space by the dancer's body, is — in our eyes, today — a fundamental element of dance. But this was not the case before the nineteenth century, when the floor pattern made in the course of a dance (together with the dance's rhythmic structure) was of far greater significance than the lines made in space by the dancer's limbs. With the evolution of costume, the lines of the body assumed greater visual importance, and the display of line became an essential element of the developing form of the classical *pas de deux*.

The man, by offering firm but discreet support to the woman, enables her to sustain her balance on *pointe*, showing the line of her movements to their greatest advantage. No matter how accomplished the woman's own

The Partner

performance, it can be ruined by weak, inept partnering. Physical strength is only one ingredient of good partnering; of equal and often greater importance are a finely judged sense of timing, an intelligent understanding of the individual female dancer's particular strengths and weaknesses, and the sense of authority that comes from real knowledge and skill. All these qualities will not only put the girl at her ease, giving her both psychological and physical support, but they will also gain the confidence of the audience.

Obviously, the close understanding and intimate rapport that characterize a truly fine dance partnership are usually to be found among couples who dance together very frequently and regularly. One of the most famous ballet partnerships of this century was that of Alicia Markova and Anton Dolin. More recently, there was that of Antoinette Sibley and Anthony Dowell. Even the incomparable Margot Fonteyn (whose main partners had been Robert Helpmann and Michael Somes) found a whole new lease on life, just as her career seemed to be drawing to a close, when she discovered a new and ideal cavalier in the young Rudolf Nureyev. Their partnership was to become one of the ballet legends of the sixties, in many ways comparable with that great partnership of showbusiness, Fred Astaire and Ginger Rogers. But ideal dance partnerships, like ideal marriages, are made in heaven. The vast majority of dancers are obliged to work with a series of different partners, and the skill required to do so successfully is acquired only through patient study and long experience.

The art of partnering can and should be taught. It is a highly specialized subject, and needs to be taught by experienced professionals. Outside the big vocational ballet schools, where *pas de deux* classes are an important part of the curriculum, there are all too few double-work classes available.

There are, of course, a number of practical considerations which make it difficult for many schools to run regular *pas de deux* classes, not the least being the necessity of having equal or similar numbers of male and female students of the appropriate standard. For classical ballet there is the added difficulty that whereas a male dancer can learn the basic elements of supported *adage* work without yet being a very accomplished classical dancer himself, there is no way a girl can attempt this until her *pointe* work is strong and her basic classical technique and placement of a fairly high standard. (Lifting, of course, should not be attempted until the boy's back is strong enough — but this will be discussed in more detail further on.)

Desmond Kelly supports Margaret Barbieri 'on balance' in this rehearsal scene from *The Two Pigeons*.

In this scene from Ashton's *Sinfonietta* danced by students of the Royal Ballet School, the girl is supported 'off balance'.

The Royal Ballet School performing Ashton's *Sinfonietta*. An example of a dance where one girl is supported by a number of dancers.

Two students, Elizabeth Morgan and David Peden, of The Royal Ballet School in another scene from Ashton's *Sinfonietta*.

If no double-work class is available, it is often possible for a group of dancers to get together and, sharing the cost of a private lesson between them, persuade a teacher to give them special coaching from time to time. Such a class need not last longer than one hour (at the most) and a ratio of two girls to each young man can work very well. This is mainly because the movements involved in supported classical *adage*, are, on the whole, more strenuous for the girl than for her partner. Of course, once it comes to lifting, the reverse is true, and here it becomes essential not to over-tax the men, as can easily happen where the numbers of men and women are not equal, or if the men are very young and therefore physically not yet fully developed.

There are young men who have the inborn instincts of a good partner. There is always something unselfish about the way a boy with a natural flair for partnering works with a girl, an approach combining strength with gentleness. His first thought is invariably to support her and present her in the best possible light, yet with sufficient self-confidence and authority: he should not carry discretion to the point of total self-effacement. Natural good manners play an important role in all this.

The *Grand Pas de Deux Classique* is the name given to the duet with solo variations traditionally performed in the big classical ballets by the *prima ballerina* and the *premier danseur*. (The term *primo ballerino*, the linguistic equivalent, for the male, of the Italian term *prima ballerina*, is very seldom used. It is generally replaced by the French term *premier danseur*, literally the 'first dancer'.) The traditional *Grand Pas de Deux* consists of five sections: the *Entrée*, the *Adage*, the Solo Variation for the *premier danseur*, the Solo Variation for the *prima ballerina* and a concluding *Coda* for both dancers together. Whenever they are together on stage, the man's full attention must be focussed on the needs of the ballerina, with no thought of saving his energies for his own solo dancing. This devotion to his partner is sensed by the audience, making them all the more receptive to the cavalier's subsequent solo performance.

In the theatre, the quality of each perfomance varies. Even the best and most experienced of ballerinas has 'off' moments, or a day when she is not really 'on form'. She is like a finely tuned musical instrument, and it is her partner's job to sense immediately if her balance is slightly out of true, and to make the necessary adjustments, anticipating and solving problems with

The Partner

split-second timing. All this obviously underlines the advantages of having a regular partner.

On the whole, this applies mainly to the intricacies of classical dance, and to the complexities presented by some of the lifts favoured by the choreographers of present-day ballet productions. But everyone knows, simply from dancing with a number of different girls or boys at a party or a disco, how one partner is so much more compatible than another (and this can be totally independent of compatibility in other spheres). This is true even of those dances, popular among young people in recent years, that involve no physical contact at all between boy and girl. How much more applicable is it then, for example, to ballroom dancing, where the man holds the woman in his arms as he leads her round the dance floor?

Professional ballroom dancers understand very well the subtleties of this relationship between two dancers, and most serious ballroom dancers will only work with their one, regular dance partner. The world of ballroom dancing, both professional and amateur, is an active and thriving one, particularly in Britain, where competition work is highly organized. However, on the whole, social dancing falls outside the scope of this book. Some information will be found in the chapter 'Dancing for Pleasure', and for those interested in learning more about this kind of dancing the Directory will give the addresses of organizations able to provide further information.

Learning to partner a girl correctly involves some things which may not come easily to young people brought up in this age of relaxed informality and an often casual approach to social behaviour. For the male dancer, standing and walking well (without slouching or prancing); knowing how to offer a girl his hand or his arm; being able to judge the appropriate distance between his partner and himself at any given moment — all these things are an indispensable part of the gentlemanly aspect of partnering. In this respect, a superficial veneer of 'period style' will do little to disguise a lack of innate good manners.

In addition to these gentlemanly qualities, the good partner needs to study and master the whole gamut of 'holds', 'grips', 'supports' and other tricks of the trade. These are the technicalities of the mechanics of double-work, as opposed to the elements of social, person to person rapport involved in a dance for two (or more) people. These two aspects of partnering must

Nicola Roberts and Phillip Broomhead demonstrating a high lift in a graduate *pas de deux* class at the Royal Ballet School.

Jennet Zerbe and Duff Harris of the California Festival Ballet, demonstrate a shoulder lift.

be made to blend seamlessly together.

The mechanics of double-work can be divided into those involved mainly in supporting the girl and those concerned with lifting her off the floor and carrying her. In ballet, the first also covers a whole technique of supported pirouettes and other turning movements.

The rules involved can and should be varied according to the girl being partnered. One will, for instance, prefer to feel the man's hands firmly supporting her waist just prior to a pirouette — another may find this hinders her in the execution of the turn.

There are many such little variations of basic partnering techniques which need to be studied and gradually, with experience, mastered by the partner. He must be versatile and adaptable and be prepared to accept that the audience (and all too often the girl) will almost invariably blame him for anything that goes wrong, sometimes totally without justification.

In recent years there has been an enormous development in the techniques of lifting, holding and carrying the female dancer. Choreographers are making more and more use of these often acrobatic — and occasionally rather dangerous — effects. Dangerous because some movements can place excessive strain on the male dancer's back, and on his neck. Extreme caution should be used when teaching young dancers to lift, hold and carry their partners.

First and foremost no boy should ever attempt to lift a girl unless he is wearing a special dance support (jockbelt or jockstrap). Secondly, no boy should be asked to do any lifting until his arms, his legs and, in particular, his back are strong enough.

Most professional ballet schools now include a carefully balanced programme of weight-lifting and other strengthening exercises in their male curriculum. In these weight-lifting exercises the emphasis should always be on achieving and maintaining the correct position and placement of the body and of the weight to be lifted, rather than aiming to lift increasingly heavier weights. As with double-work, it is not brute strength that matters (excepting perhaps for a few, specialized lifts) but accuracy and co-ordination.

It is impossible and unwise to generalize as to the age when it becomes safe for a boy to start lifting. A well-built lad, with a compact frame, can normally attempt work that would be well beyond the range of a gangly

The Partner

youth, who is in a period of rapid growth, even though the latter may be the older of the two. Much depends on common sense, but in these matters it is always better to err on the side of caution. Growing boys can very easily injure their backs and their knees by lifting too soon (or too much), and this could permanently jeopardize their careers. Absence of body hair (in particular pubic hair) can normally be taken as an absolute sign that the boy is not yet ready to start lifting; but the reverse is not necessarily true.

The most spectacular lifts are not always the hardest to do. Getting a girl up above his head, at arm's length, takes strength and careful timing on the man's part — but holding her there, once his elbows are locked in position, requires less strength than is needed, for instance, to carry her along at chest level. The height of a lift is secondary to the degree of control exercised.

There are a number of different ways of lifting a girl, but the only way to bring her down is carefully and gently onto one foot (or both, as dictated by the choreography); often this descent will be onto the tips of her toes; carelessness could result in the girl breaking her foot or sustaining some other serious injury. So the care and consideration shown towards his partner has wider implications for the male dancer than those concerned merely with the gentlemanly manners of a classical *pas de deux*.

Nowadays, of course, we find various choreographic examples of a number of men partnering one girl; of girls supporting other girls; of men lifting other men. Sometimes these are merely gimmicks, sometimes they have a real artistic validity. But the essence of double-work still remains that of the male–female relationship, be it in the form of a romantic love duet, a formalized ritual of courtship or a battle of the sexes. So the ability to act, to communicate emotion and feeling both to each other and to the audience, be it gentle tenderness, stylized eroticism, or unbridled passion, forms an essential part of the dancer's professional skills. And this applies whether or not he is even on speaking terms with his partner off stage!

If I have spoken mostly about double-work in relation to ballet, it is because ballet, in both its classical and its contemporary forms, makes a much more comprehensive, varied and complex use of partnering in all its aspects than does any other form of dance. This is exemplified by much of Kenneth MacMillan's choreography, known to many people through the highly successful televising of his ballet, *Mayerling*.

Showbusiness in this, as in all matters, uses anything and everything that will produce the desired effect for a particular number; the fashion of the day is much more relevant here than aesthetic or stylistic considerations or traditions. But whereas both in ballet and in showbusiness, some movements (in double-work as well as in solos or group dancing) will be used, legitimately and unashamedly, to display virtuosity, or to create an effect of showmanship, choreographers working in modern and contemporary dance disciplines normally strive to integrate all movements into the organic structure of a dance, eschewing the use of effects for their own sake. Consequently the range and extent of the double-work techniques used by many modern dance groups is generally more limited and less spectacular and highly specialized than those found in ballet companies. But here, too, we find increasing cross-fertilization between modern dance and ballet — exemplified by the work of choreographers like Glen Tetley — continually expanding the limits of what is expected of professional dancers. The specialized area of contact-improvisation has already been mentioned in Chapter Four.

Two graduate students of the Royal Ballet School, Nicola Roberts and Phillip Broomhead, demonstrate a one-handed lift.

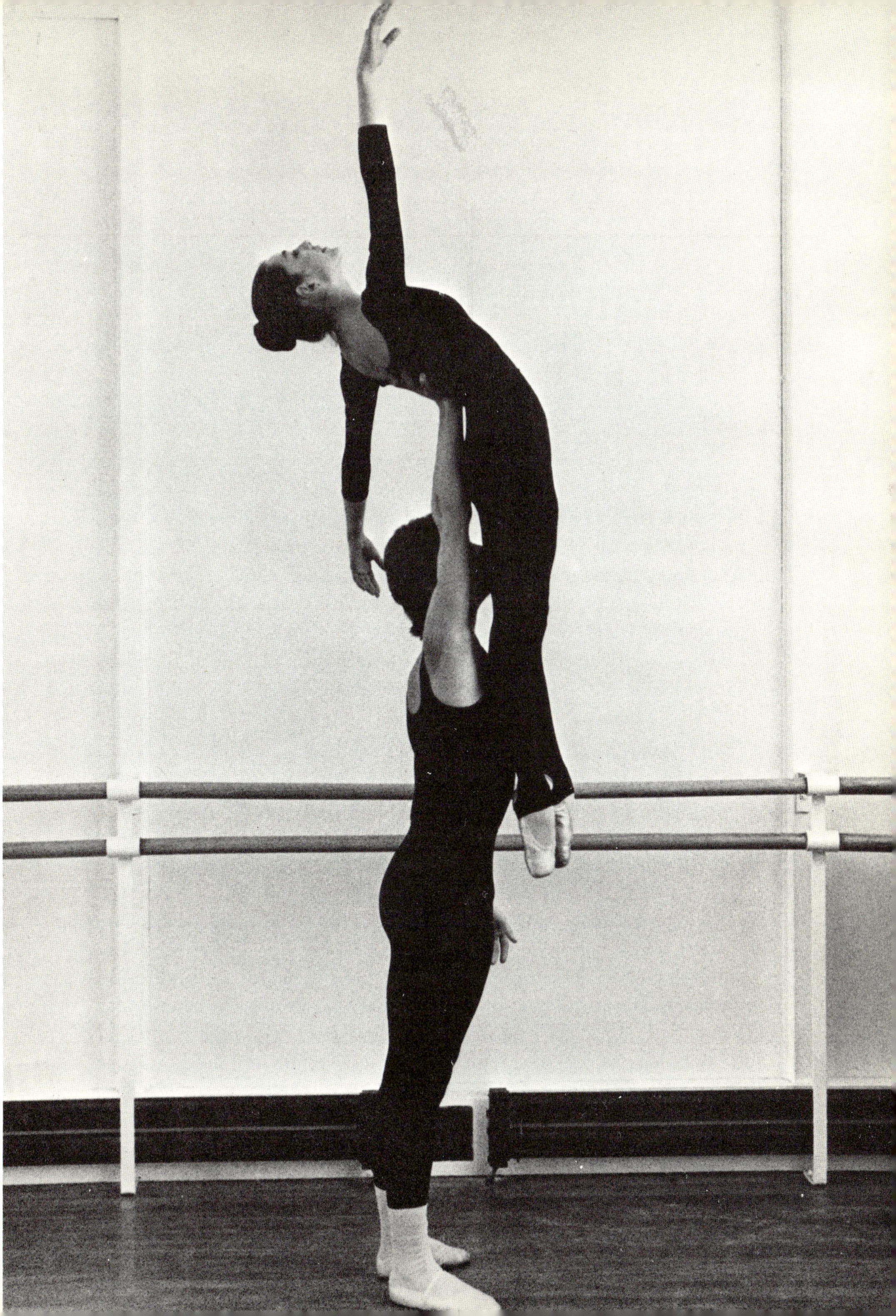

7

WORKING CONDITIONS AND CAREER PROSPECTS

All over the world, more and more young men are entering the dancing profession. Standards have risen rapidly in recent years and there is growing competition for a wide variety of jobs for male dancers.

Whether it be contemporary dance, jazz or classical ballet, dancing is now widely accepted and increasingly respected as a career for men.

Inevitably there are some fringe groups, of one kind or another leading a hand-to-mouth existence; but the able, well-trained male dancer employed by one of the many established companies, now enjoys the same living standards as anyone else, with properly structured salary scales, medical benefits, pension schemes, paid holidays, etc. Earnings are at least comparable to, and in some cases better than, average salaries for many skilled jobs or managerial and professional occupations.

Whilst it is true, in strictly financial terms, that no dancer — other than a handful of top stars — is likely to become a very rich man, it is equally true (and surely more important?) that the satisfaction of doing a job one really loves provides ample compensation for some limitation in financial rewards.

To summarize details given elsewhere about working conditions in the three main categories of professional work:

Good ballet dancers are usually attached to a permanent company, often (but not necessarily) resident in an opera house or major theatre, and enjoying a state or municipal subsidy. They will be members of a union and are normally assured of secure and regular employment, in some cases enjoying all the benefits of a state employee. Contracts are normally on a yearly basis and promotion is based on a hierarchical system (*corps de ballet, coryphee*, soloist, principal).

Dancers working in showbusiness, on the other hand, lead a more precarious existence; invariably free-lance, once they start to emerge from the chorus they need the services of a good agent to help them secure the best jobs in an increasingly competitive and fast-moving area of the profession. Union protection is effective and although (as opposed to most ballet companies) continuity of employment is not assured, the financial rewards can be much higher. This is particularly true of film and television work.

Less secure are those dancers working for some of the smaller contemporary dance groups. With a few very notable exceptions, modern dance groups do tend to lack the establishment recognition and the relative financial security now widely enjoyed by ballet companies. Nor do they have the commercial potential of showbusiness. But as the popularity of contemporary dance increases, so does the possibility of job security for the performers.

Of course, job security is probably the last thing most dedicated dancers think about. Otherwise they would be doing a cosy, nine-to-five job, instead of putting themselves through the hours of often gruelling hard physical and mental work, day in day out, which all dancers have to do throughout both their training and their entire career.

Because it is so often part of the dancer's job to make his work appear effortless and fun to do, many people seem to think of dancing as a frivolous, almost simplistic occupation. Once they are made even partially aware of the enormously hard work involved, they sometimes tend to regard dancers as slightly odd for willingly subjecting themselves to such long and arduous labours in return for such apparently limited rewards. The thing that is so hard for the non-dancer to really understand is that the true reward and purpose of dancing lies largely in the work itself; in the physical and emotional satisfaction the dancer derives from dancing, and from communicating these emotions and this physicality to an audience.

But although, as I have said, the dedicated dancer is more concerned with dancing than with considerations of job security, there are nonetheless two inescapable facts of life he must face: the possibility of his career being seriously interrupted or even terminated, at any time, by physical injury;

and the inevitability of not being able to pursue a very active dancing career much beyond middle-age.

Let me deal first with the question of injuries. To some extent these are, of course, an occupational hazard all dancers have to learn to live with; but considering the stresses and contortions to which every dancer subjects his body in the course of a normal day's work, it is amazing how free from serious injury most dancers remain. Nevertheless, we must accept that accidents do happen and that an injury which, in the context of most other occupations, might be considered a minor one, and therefore no impediment to continued work, could spell the end of a dancer's career.

We can dismiss this gloomy possibility as merely 'a risk one has to take' — and that risk is not great. But there still remains the reality that dancing is mainly a *young* man's occupation.

Few dancers continue an active career much beyond the age of forty. Some (particularly in those ballet companies performing a more traditional repertoire of narrative works) will continue for many years as character artists and mimes; so an ability to act, to create and sustain a characterization and to understand subtleties of style and period are a considerable asset, particularly to the older dancer. As, indeed, the ability to speak lines and to sing will help sustain and prolong a dancer's career in showbusiness. As they grow older, some dancers gradually move into other areas of the theatrical profession. This can occasionally entail a degree of retraining but generally, as in so much to do with the theatre, it is more a matter of being in the right place at the right time, having the necessary contacts, and learning to recognize and seize any good opportunity that comes along.

Choreography offers further career opportunities for a few talented (and lucky) young men; but no matter how gifted, not many will be able to earn their livings purely as choreographers, such posts are more often than not combined with that of ballet master. The choreographer's job is to create new ballets, whereas the ballet master directs rehearsals of existing works. Every major opera house has such a post.

Alternatively, for the dancer with the necessary aptitude, working as a dance notator or choreologist, the person who records choreography in the form of notation, offers particularly interesting opportunities for a second career, and one in which he can make full use of his professional knowledge as a dancer. There are various forms of dance notation, the Benesh and the

Working Conditions and Career Prospects

Laban methods being among those most widely used (see Directory). The rudiments of one of these methods are taught in many professional dance schools.

A number of dancers approaching retirement consider the possibility of changing to teaching. This can often provide a secure and satisfying second career, but it is also one which should not be embarked upon unless the person concerned has the necessary patience and sense of vocation to be a good teacher.

Various retraining schemes exist for dancers who want to become teachers (see Directory for details); but often the best course of action is to become apprenticed to an already experienced teacher with an established school.

Of course, this will almost invariably involve teaching children, a very different matter from training professional students. Teaching a professional company is different again. This is often one of the duties of a company's resident ballet master.

If he ends up running his own school, the ex-dancer will also need a general knowledge and understanding of basic business practices.

What of those dancers who don't become teachers or choreographers, and who lack either the ability or the desire (or, indeed, the opportunity) to branch out into some other field of theatre? Sooner or later, they will have to face up to changing to a totally different occupation. That could entail taking some sort of training course, so the better the young man's general education, the easier this could prove to be.

Provided he is realistic about it and equips himself as well as possible for it, there is no reason at all why changing careers in his mid-thirties (or thereabouts) need seem a daunting prospect to a dancer reaching the end of his active dancing career. Most dancers make this change successfully. The self-discipline and the capacity for hard work characteristic of his profession will be two important factors in the ex-dancer's favour. Often, his dancing career will have taken him on extensive tours both abroad and throughout his own country, so that he will have learnt to work in all sorts of circumstances and to get on with many different kinds of people. And his dancing will usually have kept him fitter than most men of his age.

Above all, he will have spent anything from fifteen to twenty-five years working with like-minded people at something they really cared about and which, in most cases, will have brought them a great deal of satisfaction and fulfilment.

Examples that spring immediately to mind of four male dancers of my own acquaintance who have successfully changed course after a career in dancing are of one who has become a chef, with his own restaurant; one who is now a well-known designer; one who deals in property (buying old houses and re-decorating them for re-sale); and one who is a successful television director. And there are many other excellent examples, including dancers who have gone on to university.

This may seem an unconventional way for a young man to plan for his future, but it can also be a stimulatingly challenging one; a challenge no aspiring dancer need fear to meet.

The specific requirements for becoming a professional dancer have been dealt with elsewhere, but I would conclude this chapter by pointing out that this is a profession open to anyone of the right age, the required physical attributes and the necessary talent, regardless of social or educational background and, indeed, regardless of race.

Of course, some works are part and parcel of a specific cultural heritage and tradition — be it European, Asian or African — and therefore do not easily lend themselves to being performed by dancers from a totally different ethnic background; but basically dance itself knows no barriers of nationality or race, any more than it knows barriers of language: it is itself the most universal of all languages. The polyglot constitution of so many dance audiences, as of so many dance companies, is the best possible proof of that.

8

A DAY IN THE LIFE OF A PROFESSIONAL DANCER

The day I had picked to ask Stephen Sheriff to talk to me about his usual routine as a member of the Royal Ballet Company had turned out to be rather more eventful than a dancer's average working day. For one thing, after nearly four years in the *corps de ballet,* he had just been chosen to understudy the Bluebird in *The Sleeping Beauty* — one of the most desirable male solo roles in the classical repertory, as well as one of the most difficult and strenuous to dance. Michael Somes had already started coaching him and, that very afternoon, Dame Ninette de Valois herself had watched the rehearsal.

It is unusual for such a comparatively young and inexperienced dancer to be asked to understudy as important a role as the Bluebird. Because of illness and injury among the more senior artists of the company, the management were having to draw on their reserves and, for Stephen, this might prove to be the lucky break every dancer hopes for.

As we sat discussing his good fortune over a very early dinner, just around the corner from the Opera House where he had a performance later that evening, Stephen was recognized and congratulated by the waiter, who had seen him dancing the previous week. Another indication of success and possibly fame to come? Perhaps — but probably no more than a mere coincidence. Dancers don't have much time for this kind of romantic speculation; they are too busy with everyday practicalities, like the fact that Stephen could not allow himself to eat too much so soon before a show, and that although he was due to appear only in the last ballet on the programme that evening, he still had to be in the theatre no later than 7 p.m., the statutory half-hour before curtain-up.

His day had started earlier than usual. Company class is not until 10.30 a.m., but that day, as he put it, 'I was feeling dedicated, so I joined an extra class with the graduate boys at the School.' The Royal Ballet School and the Royal Ballet Company share a large studio complex at Barons Court, in West London — a fifteen-minute tube ride from the Royal Opera House at Covent Garden, and Stephen was taking the opportunity of doing an extra class with a visiting American teacher. Also there, even at that early hour, were two of the company's senior ballerinas. Even top dancers never stop studying.

Getting to West London, from his home in Stepney, in time for that 9 a.m. class, had meant rising at 7.15 a.m. 'I normally get eight hours' sleep, but tend to feel better for the rest of the day if I sleep only seven hours and make myself get up early. Meal times in this business can be very erratic and you find yourself surviving on junk food, so I always start the day with a cooked breakfast, which, luckily, my mother prepares for me.'

Stephen still lives with his parents but is now in the process of buying his own house. He views with mixed feelings the prospect of those household chores which will soon have to be fitted into an already very full day.

After his extra, early class with the graduate students, Stephen has time for a quick cup of coffee 'with four sugars, to keep me going' before starting his official class with the other men in the company. This lasts until 11.45 a.m., so today he will have put in two and a half hours of hard training before his day of rehearsing and performing has even begun.

Company class is followed by a fifteen minutes break. Time to grab another sugary coffee, and to scan the notice board. All rehearsal and performance duties are posted on the board at the beginning of each week, but any necessary amendments or alterations are added, day by day, in red. 'I rush to the notice board straight after class each day, hoping to find I've suddenly been given an interesting new role to learn, or an unexpected performance of a part I've been understudying. This can be the most exciting moment of the day — like when I found I was down to learn Bluebird. Fantastic!'

At twelve o'clock rehearsals begin. They continue until 3 p.m. if there is a performance that evening; if not, they go on until about 5 p.m.

A Day in the Life of a Professional Dancer

'It's best if you're first cast for something, because then you're really dancing full-out at the rehearsal. For the second cast, going through the steps at the back of the studio, it can be crowded and a little frustrating at times. And if you're not even second cast, but only the understudy, you have to resist the temptation to just sit and watch the others dancing the role. There are often long periods with nothing to do, just waiting for your turn. Then you have to wrap yourself in wool to keep your muscles warm and ready for work when the ballet master calls for you.'

During these periods of inactivity the dancers often slip down to the physiotherapist's room. There's usually a strained muscle or other minor injury requiring the help of some massage, heat lamp or ultra-sonic ray treatment. 'And even if there's nothing wrong with you, you tend to drift into the physio room for a chat.'

On those days when there is a rehearsal on the stage at the Opera House, there is a warm-up class in the theatre at 9.45 a.m. Because of the lack of space and facilities at Covent Garden, the *corps de ballet* often have to warm-up as best they can on the carpeted floor of the foyer, a situation very familiar to any dancer who has done much touring.

Stage calls normally start at 10.45 a.m. (a little earlier for dress rehearsals) and continue until lunch time. Then it's back to Barons Court for further rehearsals in the studio until the end of the afternoon. After that there are often costume fittings to attend and many dancers are also involved in extra rehearsal, in their free time, as part of the regular performances of experimental choreography staged by the Royal Ballet Choreographic Group. In this way, any member of the company interested in choreography has an opportunity of showing creative work.

After his gruelling Bluebird rehearsal this afternoon, Stephen had spent an hour rehearsing for a new ballet being choreographed by a young colleague, and due to be performed in a few weeks' time at a Sunday evening workshop performance. All this is extra, voluntary work, as was his appearance a few weeks earlier, together with many other performers, at a Sunday-night Charity Gala. 'That was exhausting with extra rehearsals, lasting sometimes till 8 p.m. — but it was great fun, too, particularly doing a special number with rock star Freddy Mercury of "Queen".

There are free evenings, when it's an opera night at Covent Garden or if you're not involved at all in a particular ballet programme. But even if

Stephen Sheriff at the barre in company class with the Royal Ballet.

Stephen Sheriff relaxing between class and rehearsal.

Men of the Royal Ballet in company class.

'Rehearsals inevitably involve periods of sitting around, awaiting your turn.' Dancers of the Sadler's Wells Royal Ballet sit at the side of the stage, waiting and watching.

you're only understudying, you have to report to the theatre at the half-hour. If I'm definitely down to dance, I get there much earlier — about 6 p.m.

After checking the notice board at the stage-door for any last-minute alterations, I go down to the canteen for a coffee (with four lumps of sugar!). I don't eat anything after about six o'clock, not until I get home after the show. Because of the redevelopment at the Opera House, dressing-room accommodation is limited at present. The men in the *corps de ballet* and the *coryphees* (they're on the next step up the hierarchical ladder) have to share a dressing room, anything up to twenty of us together. We each have a locker, but apart from that we can't leave anything in the dressing room as it is also used on opera nights by singers in the opera chorus.

I always start by putting on my stage make-up. That takes no more than fifteen or twenty minutes for a 'straight' make-up, longer if I'm playing a character role. The ballet master is available by request for anyone who wants a warm-up class before the show; otherwise we do our own warm-up backstage. After warming-up, I go back to the dressing room, check my costume, which has been laid out by the dresser, make any necessary adjustments to my make-up and then get dressed and go down on stage. When I'm not on in a ballet, or in a particular act, I usually watch from the wings, especially if I'm understudying one of the roles involved.

At the end of the show there are the curtain calls; these are directed by the stage manager and it's very exciting if he gives you a 'red runner' — that means you get to go out in front of the curtain, the 'red runner', in front of which the soloists take their bows after the general company calls.

Then it's back to the dressing room and off with the costume and make-up as quickly as possible, and home to a bath and a meal.

I don't go to parties during the week, unless it's an official reception of some sort. I need my sleep. On Sundays I just collapse. Actually, I usually go to church twice on Sundays. I find it very relaxing and therapeutic.'

There's not a lot of time for socializing in a professional dancer's busy life. There are always dozens of little things that need to be done: practice tights to wash, shoes to attend to, a particularly tricky step to be practised. A lot of extra work is done outside of official rehearsal times, working out a move with a new dance partner, or pondering the interpretation of a new role.

Most of Stephen's friends are other dancers in the company, but he does

A Day in the Life of a Professional Dancer

have the advantage of being able to get right away from theatre life at weekends when he takes part in the social life at the East End Mission, in Stepney, which is run by his father.

Stephen was born in 1958 in the Turk and Caicos Islands, where his father was stationed as a Methodist missionary and his mother worked as a teacher. When he was four years old, the family moved to Jamaica, where he lived until the age of nine, when they returned to live in England.

Until then, not only had he not had any dancing lessons, he was not even consciously aware of the existence of the professional world of the theatre. 'All I did was play on the beach and enjoy the sunshine', as it turned out, an ideal start in life for a future dancer, helping to develop the strong, healthy, agile body so essential in this profession.

In England, at the local junior school in Rayleigh, Essex, Stephen took part in the general music and movement classes and in country dancing taught there by a Mrs Olive Littlejohn. Struck by the boy's natural aptitude for movement, she suggested he take tap dancing lessons. One was enough; Stephen hated it. Undeterred, Mrs Littlejohn suggested ballet lessons and, aged eleven, he started learning ballet with Miss Vicki French and was immediately enthusiastic. He was having only one lesson a week, but progressed so well that his teacher was soon able to enter him for his R.A.D. Grade I ballet examination, which he passed with honours. This encouraged his parents to take him up to London to audition for the Royal Ballet Lower School, at White Lodge. He was successful and became a boarder there in the year in which he turned thirteen.

In 1976, after three years at White Lodge and two at the Upper School, he graduated into the Royal Ballet Company. For the first eighteen months he toured the country with 'Ballet for All', an educational unit performing at schools and in the smaller theatres all over England. After this initial apprenticeship, he became a member of the *corps de ballet* of the resident company at the Royal Opera House, Covent Garden.

For his graduation performance from the Upper School, Stephen was to dance the leading role of Franz in *Coppèlia* at the school's annual matinee at the Opera House. It turned out to be a big success, in spite of the fact that, only weeks before he had been encased in plaster from chest to waist, suffering from a back injury. His student days were dogged with such difficulties; at White Lodge he fell in class, fracturing his foot. No sooner had he recovered than he fell down the stairs at Richmond Station, fracturing the other foot.

His early days in the company were unhappy. Bursting to dance, he was frustrated by not yet having sufficiently interesting or numerous dancing roles. 'I was terribly unhappy and decided to audition for the musical show *A Chorus Line,* then due to start rehearsing with an English cast. The auditions were at Drury Lane, just around the corner from the Royal Opera House. I didn't want anyone from the Royal Ballet to know what I was up to, so I would go to the auditions secretly, in a taxi. I got through to the finals and would have got into the show, but couldn't break my contract with the Royal Ballet.' Knowing Stephen had never studied jazz or modern dance, much less singing and acting, I wondered how he had managed to qualify for such a slick West End show. 'Our church organist gave me a few singing lessons,' he said disarmingly, 'and as for the dancing and the acting — they just seemed to come naturally.' Which goes to prove that the combination of natural talent and a sound ballet training are as good a basis as any for a possible career in showbusiness. In the end he became firm friends with many of the dancers in the cast of *A Chorus Line* and went to see the show fourteen times. 'I learnt so much from these people, from their professionalism, their vitality, and above all their passionate dedication to the theatre.'

Stephen doesn't keep a diary but he does write down exciting events that happen in his life, such as this brief flirtation with showbusiness, or that thrilling moment when his colleagues applauded spontaneously in the rehearsal studio the first time they saw him perform an important role which he had been understudying. And now that latest excitement, being chosen to understudy the role of the Bluebird. Stephen's days of frustration at not having enough to dance would seem to be at an end. With good luck and a lot of hard work, he could be set for a successful career in the Royal Ballet Company at Covent Garden.

Ronald Emblen in his dressing room at the Royal Opera House demonstrates the application of a character stage make-up.

The Westminster Morris Men
performing in London under the direction of
their squire, Colin Fleming.

9

DANCING FOR PLEASURE; EDUCATIONAL DANCE; AND DANCE AS THERAPY OR AS AN AID TO SPORT

So far we have concentrated on male dancing in its various professional aspects. There also exists a vast and thriving area of amateur theatre dance, but studying one of these stage techniques is not necessarily a good idea for someone wanting to learn dancing purely for pleasure.

Of the ever increasing numbers of students attending ballet schools, tap classes, jazz studios and other similar establishments all over the world, some are undoubtedly there just for the fun of it, with never a thought of dancing professionally. Unfortunately there are also far too many stage-struck hopefuls working away at a dance technique, ostensibly as a hobby, but with one eye firmly on the professional or semi-professional prospects. They sometimes find themselves caught in a vicious circle of technique classes, dance examinations and competition work, occasionally (alas) encouraged more than they ought to be by a less than scrupulous teacher. More girls than boys get themselves into this sort of situation, but male dance students are by no means immune. It can be an expensive business, and it is hard work without necessarily being very much fun.

Dancing ought to be a source of pleasure and almost anyone can attempt it in some form. If a boy can learn to catch a ball, or swim, or jump a hurdle, there is no reason why he shouldn't be able to dance a little. Deciding what kind of dance activity to take part in will depend on his age and on what is available locally (there are often more opportunities for the young adult than for the schoolboy). He must also consider *why* he wants to dance and what he hopes to get out of it.

There are many reasons for learning to dance: as a social accomplishment and a means of getting together with other people; as an aid to gymnastics or skating; to become a more informed member of the audience; as an extension of amateur theatricals; as an area of remedial work, both mental and physical; or simply as a pleasant way of keeping fit and indulging in the sheer joy of movement and rhythm.

Apart from countless private teachers and commercial schools teaching dance, classes are also held at many community centres, as well as at evening institutes and other adult education centres. Numerous college seminars and vacation courses have classes open to people of varying degrees of experience and ability, including introductory courses for adult beginners. Information about all this is normally available at public libraries, through arts associations or from local education officers. Circumstances vary widely, but an example of the sort of opportunity that does exist is provided by the dance programme offered in London, at the time of writing, by the Chelsea–Westminster Adult Education Institute. This includes ballet technique (beginners as well as elementary and intermediate standards); ballet limbering; ballroom and Latin American; modern dance (various levels); creative dance; old time dancing for the retired; old time dancing for the blind; tap dancing (beginners to advanced); Scottish country dancing and English, Irish, Hungarian, Polish and Greek dancing, as well as various dance workshop activities, including performing opportunities.

If keeping fit is the main objective, the thing to do is to seek out a studio advertising 'body conditioning' classes. These can vary from simplified balletic and modern dance exercises to rather more sophisticated courses involving the use of special apparatus.

As a specific aid to improved standards of performance for sportsmen and athletes in general, dance has much to offer. For this purpose, one of the most useful forms of dance to study is classical ballet. Quite apart from any aesthetic considerations (the controlled elegance of ballet is of obvious and particular use to the skater and the gymnast), the academic basis of classical ballet technique rests on such sound anatomical principles that — carefully and correctly taught — the exercises involved cannot but develop strength and flexibility, increase speed and stamina, and above all, improve balance and co-ordination; a boon to any athlete or sportsman.

Then there is the whole area of amateur theatrical presentations. Some of the plays staged by local drama groups involve a certain amount of

The Westminster Morris Men rehearsing in
London under the direction of Colin Fleming.

dance, and many operatic societies require dancers for amateur and semi-professional performances of operas, operettas and musical shows. Young people interested in this kind of dancing will, of course, need to study theatre dance techniques, preferably in a good commercial school offering a variety of styles.

Those wishing mainly to become better informed members of the audience will want to experience the practical side of theatre dance by attending classes for amateurs (in much the same way as the would-be amateur performer) as well as studying subjects such as dance history.

Most of the historical dancing seen on stage both in professional and amateur productions is not authentic. Sometimes it is very effective and, so long as it does not claim to be the real thing, it does no harm. But a number of individuals and organizations have devoted much time and study to the reconstruction and understanding of the authentic dances of past centuries. This can provide a fascinating subject of study for the intelligent amateur.

The Imperial Society of Teachers of Dancing (I.S.T.D.) has a flourishing Historical Dance Branch. An excellent introduction to Historical Dance has been published by the British Broadcasting Corporation (*May I have the pleasure? The Story of Popular Dancing* by Belinda Quirey, obtainable from the B.B.C., 35, Marylebone High Street, London, W1M 4AA. This publication also includes excellent sections on Rock Dance and on Morris Dancing by Steve Bradshaw and Ronald Smedley respectively).

In the same way as music, art and drama are considered an integral part of the educative process, dance is now playing an increasingly accepted and important role in education, both at school and college levels. A few universities even offer degree courses in dance, either as a separate discipline, or as part of a wider-ranging performing arts degree. For example the Faculty of Fine Arts in York University (Ontario, Canada) offers a theory-orientated B.A. (Hons.) degree and a performance-orientated B.F.A. (Hons.) course. In addition to performance, choreography and teaching skills, the Dance Department concentrates on history, criticism, notation and dance therapy. One of the oldest established Dance Departments anywhere in the world is a part of the Faculty of Music in the University of Cape Town. This offers a three-year teacher's course in ballet; less theory-orientated than most American and Canadian equivalents, it enjoys a particularly fine reputation in the teaching and performance aspects of dance. In England, the Laban Centre for Movement and Dance in the University of London Goldsmiths' College offers Dance Theatre and Dance Education courses, including a three-year B.A. Hons. and a three to four-year B.Ed. Hons. as well as Research Dance Degrees at M.Phil. and Ph.D. levels. A majority of colleges in the U.S.A. offer dance studies of some kind and there are an increasing number of such courses available in Britain. Local education authorities will provide information about the latter and the *Dance Magazine Directory of Dance in Colleges and Universities* is a useful source of information for dance programmes in America. Nearly all such institutions run extensive vacation programmes for the non-specialist. The emphasis is usually on modern dance techniques.

Many ordinary schools include some form of dance either as part of their extra-curricular activities or, increasingly, as a school subject; but a lot of silly prejudice against boys dancing still deters people (including many educationalists, who should know better) from encouraging the

A class in
Dalcroze eurhythmics
at the Whitgate
Nursery School
in London.

participation of male pupils. The greatest authority on dance in education was the late Rudolf Laban. His theories and ideas have been one of the major influences on the teaching of dance in schools, particularly in Britain. In many English schools, dance is taught as part of the Physical Education programmes, alas not always as imaginatively and efficiently as it might be. The well-intentioned but sometimes misguided efforts made, over the years, to divorce dance teaching in schools completely from the balletic aspects of theatre dance have, in many cases, resulted in too narrow a view of the subject becoming the accepted norm. In some countries ballet is now an ordinary school subject, along with music and art. For instance in England now ballet examinations can be taken at 'O' level.

For the very young child, Dalcroze eurhythmics, a method of learning music through movement, is an excellent way to start dancing. Later, the pros and cons of studying a formal dance technique, like ballet, become a matter of individual preference and priorities; but for the very young child, creative dance styles are undoubtedly of greater value than imitative ones.

There is a growing awareness in medical circles of the therapeutic possibilities of dance. Movement studies can be of help not only in the rehabilitation of some accident victims and in ensuring the general physical and mental well-being of the handicapped, but also in the treatment of behavioural problems. Dance therapy is a subject frequently included as part of a university or college general dance course, often in conjunction with psychology studies. It is a field where a great deal of interesting work is being done by people operating on the fringe of conventional medical and educational disciplines. Others, with no erudite pretensions but with a strong commitment to helping those less fortunate than themselves, do a fine job in the area of dance tuition for the disabled. 'Dance for people with disabilities' is an I.S.T.D. and Disabled Living joint project catering for the mentally handicapped, the physically handicapped, the blind, the deaf and the emotionally disturbed. (See Directory for address.)

A generation ago, when formal ballroom dancing was still in vogue, learning to dance was a very necessary social accomplishment for every young man and woman. In the rapidly changing social scene of the years following World War II, with a general freedom from convention manifesting itself more and more in every walk of life, social dancing went through a rapid succession of new fads. Young people still danced in couples,

Gregory Bayda (left) and Marcella Cenaiko and Bohdan Zerebecky (below), students at the Natasha Lisakova School of Dance, in North London, performing Theatrical Folk Dances in the Ukranian style.

but the degree of contact between them was gradually reduced to a minimum and the set patterns and routines of ballroom dancing were replaced by a much freer, more improvised way of dancing. Within the rough limits of each new fashion, everyone did their own thing. So the process of learning to dance as a social accomplishment ceased to be a major issue. But with the nostalgia boom in full swing, a return to a more formal type of social dance might well be likely. Even without this, ballroom dancing retains a devoted following of young and old in many countries. Competition work is of an impressively high standard, particularly in Britain. Roseland, in New York and the Café de Paris in London are two of several places where afternoon *thé dansants* continue to give pleasure to many, and ballroom classes are still big business.

Urbanization and television were probably the two biggest nails in the coffin of folk dance, but even in the big cities, folk dance continues to be a source of great pleasure to many men and women. Organizations like the English Folk Dance and Song Society, the Scottish Country Dance Society and other smaller bodies have given new life to old traditions, mainly in the British Isles and the Commonwealth countries but also as far from 'home' as Boston and New York.

There are those who see so-called 'natural dance' (a form which emphasizes an improvisatory approach to dance, with the accent on communal participation) as a modern extension of folk dance. This is perhaps true in as much as this kind of dancing grew out of, and reflects some aspects of current social thinking. But it seems to me that our ancient heritage of national dance can still have vital relevance to our lives today. Many immigrant communities from countries as diverse as Turkey, Thailand and the Ukraine, to name but three, preserve and practise the dances of their homeland and are usually glad to teach them to others. It is well worth making contact with such groups and investigating the possibilities.

10

DIRECTORY OF PRACTICAL INFORMATION AND USEFUL ADDRESSES

1. PROFESSIONAL SCHOOLS

It is not possible to recommend individual private schools and studios. The schools listed below are either the official national ballet school of the country concerned, or an established institution of similar status and international reputation, *closely linked to a major dance company.*

The Royal Ballet School
Upper School   155, Talgarth Road, London W14 9DE, England
A day school for students aged sixteen to eighteen years.
Lower School   White Lodge, Richmond Park, Surrey, England
A boarding and day school for children aged eleven to sixteen years. Detailed information about the Royal Ballet School will be found in Chapter Three.

The Junior Associates of the Royal Ballet School
The Junior Associates are pupils aged eight to ten years who attend special classes, once or twice a week, at the Royal Ballet School. Classes are also held at Sadler's Wells. The object of these classes is to assess the child's potential for full-time professional training; they do not operate in competition with private dancing schools, and children already taking dancing lessons attend the Junior Associate classes as an additional part of

their training. However, it is not necessary to have had any dance training at all to join the Junior Associates. There are special boys' classes. Further information can be obtained by writing to The Royal Ballet Upper School at the address listed above.

The Rambert School of Ballet   Mercury Theatre, 2, Ladbroke Road, London W11 3NG, England

The Rambert Academy   West London Institute of Higher Education, Gordon House, 300, St Margaret's Road, Twickenham, Middlesex TW1 1PT, England

The Rambert School of Ballet is one of the oldest established professional dance schools in England, and the Mercury Theatre was the cradle of British Ballet. The School, which now operates partly from its old premises at the Mercury, and partly from new studios at The Place (17, Duke's Road, London WC1H 9AB), offers a full, professional ballet training, but there are no residential facilities, and general schooling no longer forms part of the curriculum.

In recent years, the Ballet Rambert company has become increasingly modern dance orientated and, in keeping with this changed image, a new venture was started in 1979: The Rambert Academy. This collaboration between the West London Institute of Higher Education and the Ballet Rambert provides a two-year foundation course in dance for pupils aged sixteen and over. In addition to a full dance programme (covering both modern dance and ballet) the educational facilities of the Institute enable students to study for their G.C.E. 'A' levels.

The London School of Contemporary Dance   17, Duke's Road, London WC1H 9AB, England

Recognized by the Department of Education and Science as a College of Further Education, the School is part of Contemporary Dance Trust, together with the London Contemporary Dance Theatre and the experimental theatre at The Place. This school occupies a unique position in the field of modern dance training. For further information see Chapter Four.

Directory of Practical Information

The School of American Ballet   144 West 66th Street, New York, N.Y. 10023, U.S.A.

This is the official school of the New York City Ballet Company. It is a day school, but arrangements can usually be made with private families to board teenage pupils from outside the New York area. Auditions are held in New York throughout the school year, and aspirants for the intensive, five-week Summer Course are chosen at regional auditions held in many cities across the U.S.A. The length of time regular students spend at the school depends on age, previous training and individual progress. Children starting at eight or nine years of age are usually taught separately in the Children's Divisions, whilst pupils of ten to fourteen years, with little or no previous training enter a special Preparatory Division. Both groups later converge for the more advanced stages of training.

The school is fee-paying, but it is essentially a non-profit educational institution devoted to the training of professional ballet dancers, and many scholarships are awarded. Secondary education to high school diploma level is provided by arrangement with The Professional Children's School (see separate entry page 111).

The American Ballet Theatre School   890 Broadway, New York, N. Y. 10003, U.S.A.

This is the official school of the American Ballet Theatre Company. It is non-residential and non-educational but offers a full professional ballet training at both junior and senior levels.

Some scholarships are available, but this is essentially a fee-paying school. Approved by the U.S. Government for students from abroad.

Ecole de danse de l'Opéra de Paris   8, Rue Scribe, Paris 75009, France

The national ballet school of France, and the oldest professional ballet school in the world. Trains dancers mainly for the Opéra ballet company. Caters almost exclusively for French nationals, but a proportion of five per cent of foreign students can be accepted. Pupils may enroll only between the ages of eight and twelve (thirteen for boys). After a trial period of three months there is an official entrance examination. Successful candidates are then accepted for a course lasting approximately six years. Training is free, but pupils are required to pass a very tough ballet examination every year in order to remain at the school. Traditionally a day school, but boarding facilities are now available for some pupils. General education takes place at the Ecole de la rue de Suresnes (up to the French B.E.P.C. standard) and then at the Lycée Racine.

The Royal Danish Ballet School   Royal Theatre, KGS. Nytrov 1050, Copenhagen K., Denmark

The official school of the Royal Danish Ballet Company, famous for its fine tradition of male dancing. Pupils enter from the age of eight, remaining until they are sixteen or seventeen, combining their dance studies with general education up to high school standard. Training is free.

The balletic traditions of the school are firmly rooted in the nineteenth century Bournonville ballets, still the core of the company's repertoire; but the scope of the training has been broadened in recent years to meet the demands made on the dancers by the increasingly international character of the ballets now performed at the Royal Theatre.

Stedelijk Instituut voor Ballet (Municipal Ballet Institute)   Lange Klarenstraat 11, Antwerp 2000, Belgium

This is the only ballet school in Belgium combining a professional ballet training with full-time general education. It is subsidized by the state and the City of Antwerp. The training is completely free, but foreign students whose parents are not resident in Belgium pay nominal fees. The school is fully integrated into the official education system of the City of Antwerp. Residential facilities are available. Pupils are accepted from the age of eight and auditions are held biannually, in June and in August. The upper age-limit for entry into the school is flexible and special arrangements can be made for promising teenage boys. About one third of the pupils are male, and the majority of the men trained here are subsequently employed by the Royal Ballet of Flanders (Koninklijk Ballet van Vlaanderen) with whom the school has very close links.

Mudra   Rue Bara 103, Brussels 1070, Belgium

Mudra is the name of the school attached to Maurice Bejart's Company, *Le*

Ballet du XXème siècle and caters for students of school-leaving age. Selection is by audition and tuition is free. All forms of dance are taught, with much emphasis on movement research in a 'total theatre' context. Students of all nationalities are eligible, but there are no residential facilities.

Centraal Dansberaad   Riauw Straat 53, The Hague, Holland

This organization will provide information about all aspects of dance in Holland. There are no fewer than six separate state schools concerned with the training of professional dancers for the various state-subsidized Dutch dance companies. Two are in Amsterdam, one in The Hague, one in Rotterdam and one each in Tilburg and Arnhem.

These schools are not residential. Educational arrangements vary in different parts of the country, but all children must complete the equivalent of three years of high school before embarking on full-time professional dance training at about fifteen years of age. Where necessary, there is close co-operation between the educational authorities and the dance academies, enabling children from the age of ten or eleven to attend daily dance classes. Many boys start considerably later. The dance academies are fee-paying, but bursaries and other forms of financial assistance are normally readily available.

The National Ballet School of Canada   111, Maitland Street, Toronto, Ontario, M4Y 1E4, Canada

The official school of the National Ballet of Canada. Pupils are admitted from the age of nine. It is a boarding school, but day students are also accepted and all pupils at the school follow a full educational programme to high school level, graduating from grade twelve with a diploma recognized by the Ministry of Education. The full course is nine years. Special timetables are arranged for talented boys older than ten years when entering the academic school and there is also a Special Ballet Course for boys between the ages of seventeen and twenty years who wish to become professional dancers. The school is fee-paying but a number of scholarships are available. A majority of the dancers in the National Ballet Company have been trained at this school, which enjoys a high international reputation for its standards of classical training. Preliminary auditions are held in all major cities in Canada between February and April. Successful candidates are required to attend a four week summer school in July for further assessment before being accepted into the school.

The Australian Ballet School   11, Mt Alexander Road, Flemington, Melbourne, Victoria, 3031, Australia

This is the Federal National School of Australia, subsidized by the Federal Government through the Australia Council. It is the official school of The Australian Ballet.

It is a senior school only, non-residential and non-educational (except for elective correspondence studies).

Students are accepted from the age of fifteen and must have completed four years of secondary education. The school relies on the excellent network of private teachers all over Australia to provide the early training. Entrance is by audition only; intake is limited.

The school is fee-paying, but students are eligible for T.E.A.S. (Tertiary Education Assistance to Students). Student assistance is also received from state governments and privately donated scholarships.

The majority of the men in The Australian Ballet Company and the state companies, including the principals, have received the major part of their training in the Australian Ballet School.

The National School of Ballet of New Zealand   74, Victoria Street, Wellington (P.O. Box 11-357), New Zealand

A day school supported by the Queen Elizabeth II Arts Council of New Zealand. Students are accepted from the age of fifteen for a two-year full-time course and are encouraged to continue academic studies where possible. Most dancers in the National Ballet Company of New Zealand are graduates of this school. Fees are only payable by overseas students, and the Queen Elizabeth II Arts Council awards a limited number of scholarships each year.

The Cape Town University Ballet School   Woolsack Drive, Rosebank, Cape, Republic of South Africa

Provides a full-time, three-year course for students aged sixteen and over.

There are two streams, one geared to performing, the other to teacher-training. Independent of, but works in very close collaboration with, the CAPAB Ballet Company. This fully professional company grew out of the old University of Cape Town Ballet Company, a student group directed by professionals, who did much to establish and promote ballet of a very high standard throughout southern Africa. Many graduates of this school have made significant contributions to ballet in Britain and elsewhere.

2. EXAMINING BODIES AND ASSOCIATIONS OF DANCING TEACHERS

A number of countries still have no state licensing system for teachers of dance, but many teachers belong to professional organizations, most of which conduct examinations and tests at amateur, professional and teacher-training levels. The majority are concerned with classical ballet and some deal also with social dance, as well as with other forms of stage dance such as tap and musical comedy dancing. On the whole, teachers of so-called 'contemporary' dance tend to be very individualistic, rejecting formal professional associations and dance examinations.

The following are some of the principal associations of dancing teachers and examining bodies (see also under Social Dance).

The Royal Academy of Dancing   48, Vicarage Crescent, London SW11 3LT, England
8, College Avenue, Upper Montclair, New Jersey 07043, U.S.A.
209/3050 Yonge Street, Toronto, Ontario M4N 2K4, Canada
Suite 701, 84 Pitt Street, Sydney, Australia
CPO Box 390, Wellington, New Zealand

An international body with headquarters in London, but branches in many other countries. Conducts examinations in classical ballet and is also involved in teacher-training, including a special course for ex-professional dancers wishing to retrain as teachers. Headquarters in London will supply information about the R.A.D.'s activities worldwide.

The Imperial Society of Teachers of Dancing   Euston Hall, Birkenhead Street, London WC1H 8BR, England

An association of dancing teachers covering many different styles of dance.

Consists of two faculties, one covering theatre dance and the other dealing with ballroom dancing.

The theatre faculty includes two separate ballet branches, the Imperial Ballet Branch and the Cecchetti Society. The headquarters of the I.S.T.D. are in London, but there are branches all over the world. Examinations and tests are conducted by both faculties in all the types of dance covered by them. See also Chapter One for details.

The Cecchetti Society   c/o. I.S.T.D., Euston Hall, Birkenhead Street, London WC1H 8BE, England

This society (which is embodied in The Imperial Society of Teachers of Dancing) is dedicated to preserving and propagating the work of Maestro Enrico Cecchetti. An Italian who worked extensively in Russia and in England, Cecchetti was one of the foremost ballet teachers of the late nineteenth and early twentieth centuries. He was principal teacher of the Diaghilev Company and numbered Nijinsky and Pavlova among his pupils. The society conducts professional examinations for dancers and teachers in the Cecchetti method of classical ballet, as well as graded tests and examinations for children.

The British Ballet Organization   39, Lonsdale Road, London SW13 9JP, England

Co-founded by Edouard Espinosa, a great teacher of the old French school who had settled in England. He codified what he termed 'operatic dancing' and was the first person to publish these graded classical ballet syllabi in English. The B.B.O. conducts ballet examinations in England and a number of other countries.

The Society for Russian Style Ballet   65, Tiverton Road, Potters Bar, Herts., England

This society conducts examinations in England and some other countries. These are not based on as detailed a syllabus as those of the societies listed above, but are concerned more with the style and general academic principles of the Russian style of classical ballet. It is difficult to define exactly what is meant by the term 'Russian style ballet'. Basically it is an amalgam of the French and Italian schools of the nineteenth century, remoulded by the instinctive Russian genius for dance. It was brought to the west in the early part of this century by the émigré Russian ballet teachers; these were former stars of the Imperial Russian Ballet, notably Preobajenska, Egorova, Kchessinska and Legat. The present-day Soviet Russian training evolved from the old Imperial traditions and was codified into a systematic course of study by the great Russian teacher, Vaganova.

The International Dance Teachers' Association   76, Bennett Road, Brighton BN2 5JL, England

The I.D.T.A. was created by mergers and amalgamations of several associations. Teachers can obtain qualifications in ballroom, Latin, sequence (old time), ballet, stage, tap and modern dance branches. Amateur tests are organized in all these branches of dancing, together with disco, modern sequence, gymnastics and rhythmic fitness.

3. TEACHER-TRAINING COURSES

There are many such courses, and it is impossible to name them individually or to make specific recommendations. They fall into three main categories: there are the three-year, full-time courses catering, on the whole, for students in their late teens or early twenties; then there are shorter, retraining courses for professional dancers reaching the end of their active dancing careers; and finally, for the more academically inclined, there are college and university courses leading to degrees in dance.

Many of the professional schools, examining bodies, and societies of dancing teachers listed above run teacher-training courses, and further information can be obtained by writing to them, or from the advertisements and articles in the specialist dance publications listed below.

4. SPECIALIST DANCE PUBLICATIONS AND TRADE NEWSPAPERS

The Dancing Times   18, Hand Court, High Holborn, London WC1N 6JF, England.

Magazine, published monthly in London. General articles and reviews about dance, mainly ballet, with special emphasis on dancing schools, mainly British but with some international coverage. Runs a book service. Contains an extensive directory of dancing schools and carries advertisements for specialist suppliers of dancewear. Very well illustrated.

Dance and Dancers   Hansom Books, P.O. Box 294, 2 and 4, Old Pye Street, London SW1P 2LR, England

Magazine, published monthly in London. Covers dance with emphasis on ballet, mainly in Britain and Europe. Concentrates on the professional theatre, with international directory of performances by dance companies. Very well illustrated. Many advertisements.

Dance Magazine   1180 Avenue of the Americas, New York, N.Y. 10036

Magazine, published monthly in New York. Very wide American and international dance coverage and comprehensive educational directory. Many advertisements. Very well illustrated.

Dance Magazine Directory of Dance in Colleges and Universities   (Published by *Dance Magazine*, address as above)

Comprehensive guide to dance in higher education, mainly in America.

Dance Magazine Annual   (Published by *Dance Magazine*, address as above)

Contains some international information, but is essentially a very comprehensive professional guide to every aspect of the American dance world, dealing with dance artists and all types of dance services, sponsors, schools, suppliers, etc.

Les Saisons de la Danse   3, Rue des Petits-Carreaux, Paris 75002, France

Monthly Parisian ballet magazine, well illustrated. Lists dancing schools all over France.

Danse   12, Rue Chabanais, Paris 75002, France

Published every six weeks, in Paris. Widest international coverage of any French-language dance magazine. Very well illustrated.

Directory of Practical Information

New Dance   X6 Dance Space, Butler's Wharf, Lafone Street, London SE1, England

Published quarterly by a Dance Collective and gives extensive coverage of fringe activities, mainly in Britain.

Time Out   Tower House, Southampton Street, London WC2E 7HD

Published weekly in London as a guide to all forms of entertainment available in and around the London area, this magazine gives excellent coverage of dance events, especially of new and experimental groups. Includes details of dance and movement courses and various fringe activities.

The Village Voice   842 Broadway, New York, N.Y. 10003, U.S.A. (Subscription address: 643 Ryan Way, Marion, Ohio 43302)

New York Weekly newspaper. Covers all aspects of the New York dance scene, including experimental work and fringe activities such as performances in lofts.

The Stage and Television Today   47, Bermondsey Street, London SE1 3XT, England

Weekly newspaper, published in London covering most aspects of the entertainments scene in Britain.

The Hollywood Drama-Logue   P.O. Box 38771, Hollywood, California 90038, U.S.A.

Published weekly in Hollywood. Includes coast-to-coast news, reviews and casting notices.

Backstage   165 West 46th Street, New York, N.Y. 10036, U.S.A.

Published weekly in New York. Extensive coverage of the showbiz scene in the U.S.A., including television and films. There is a lively Dance Diary and a special Dance Casting section.

5. METHODS OF MOVEMENT NOTATION

There are several different methods of recording movement by means of notation. Nowadays those most widely used are Labanotation and Choreology (the latter is often referred to as Benesh Notation).

Two other methods that have a fairly wide following are the Eshkol-Wachman Notation (in Israel) and the Sutton Notation (in the U.S.A.).

For those with the necessary aptitude, a professional training in this field can help provide a very desirable alternative dance career. Most major dance companies now employ the services of a choreologist or a dance notator.

Further information, including details of training courses, can be obtained from the organizations listed below.

The Dance Notation Bureau   505 Eighth Ave., New York, N. Y. 10018, U.S.A.

A library and research centre devoted to the study and propagation of most forms of movement notation and in particular Labanotation, the system of movement notation invented by Rudolf Laban. Includes a professional training school for studies in movement analysis and notation.

The Institute of Choreology Ltd   4, Margravine Gardens, London W6 8RH, England

Teaches the system of movement notation invented by Rudolf and Joan Benesh and officially called Choreology. Also houses an extensive library of dance works recorded in this method.

6. DALCROZE EURHYTHMICS

Emile Jaques-Dalcroze was a Swiss music teacher and theoretician. He devised a system for encouraging and training musical sensibility through physical movement. It provides an excellent introduction to dance training, in particular for young children. Information regarding training facilities available in various countries, both for children and at teacher-training level, can be obtained from the addresses listed below.

Institut Jaques-Dalcroze   44, Rue de la Terassière, Geneva, Switzerland

The Dalcroze Society   89, Highfield Avenue, London NW11, England

F.I.E.R. (Fédération Internationale des Enseignements de Rhythmique) c/o Van Hogen Loucklaan 32, The Hague, Holland

The Dalcroze School   161 East 73rd Street, New York, N.Y., 10021, U.S.A.

7. SOCIAL DANCE

The following organizations will provide further information about opportunities for learning various forms of social dance. See also under Examining Bodies and Associations of Dancing Teachers as listed above.

The English Folk Dance and Song Society   2, Regents Park Road, London NW1

The Scottish Country Dance Society   c/o 12, Coates Crescent, Edinburgh EH37 A5

Country Dance and Song Society of America   505 Eighth Ave., New York, N.Y. 10018

International Council of Ballroom Dancing   13, Penrhyan Road, Kingston-on-Thames KT1 2BZ, England

United States Ballroom Branch of the Imperial Society of Teachers of Dancing   154 Dow Avenue, Iselin, NJ 08830, U.S.A.

National Council of Dance Teachers Organizations   11205 South Dixie Highway, Miami, Florida 33156, U.S.A.

Many of the major ballroom dancing schools in the U.S.A. belong to this organization.

8. DANCE THERAPY AND DANCE FOR THE DISABLED

American Dance Therapy Association   Suite 230, 2000 Century Plaza, Columbia, Maryland 21044, U.S.A.

Founded in 1966 to establish and maintain high standards of professional education and competence in the field of Dance Therapy. Publications include the *American Journal of Dance Therapy* and the A.D.T.A. Newsletter.

Dance For People With Disabilities   c/o 76, St Edmunds Drive, Stanmore, Middlesex HA7 2AU, England

A joint project of the Imperial Society of Teachers of Dancing and the Disabled Living Foundation. Works in the field of dance and movement for the mentally handicapped, the physically handicapped, the blind, the deaf and the emotionally disturbed.

9. SPECIALIST BOOKSHOPS

The following are all specialist dance bookshops dealing with most published work connected with dance.

Dance Books   9, Cecil Court, London WC2N 4EZ, England

The Ballet Bookshop   1887 Broadway, New York, N.Y. 10023, U.S.A.

La Danse   14, Rue de Beaune, 75007 Paris, France

10. OTHER USEFUL ADDRESSES

The Council for Dance Education and Training   5, Tavistock Place, London WC1H 9SS

The Council has been set up to speak on behalf of dance to official organizations such as the Department of Education and Science and the local education authorities in Britain. Its wide terms of reference include the ability to recommend with authority institutions and courses which should be recognized as of good standing and worthy of government support.

American Dance Guild   1133 Broadway, Suite 1427, New York, N.Y. 10010, U.S.A.

A non-profit organization promoting and serving the art of dance. Publishes *Dance Scope*, a bi-annual review of dance in the U.S.A. with special emphasis on new developments.

Directory of Practical Information

Dance in Canada Association   100, Richmond Street East, Suite 325, Toronto, Ontario, Canada M5C 2P9

A non-profit national organization dedicated to promoting all aspects of dance in Canada. Publishes a quarterly magazine, *Dance in Canada*.

Association of Ballet Clubs   c/o 51, Vartry Road, London N15, England

Serves as a link between the many ballet clubs situated all over Britain. These are non-professional groups of ballet lovers who meet regularly to share in various activities connected with dance, such as lectures, film shows and occasional stage productions. The Association is able to offer advice, help to co-ordinate activities, and generally promote the interests of member clubs. It organizes an Annual Production in London and issues a Bulletin.

National Association for Regional Ballet   1860 Broadway, New York, N.Y. 10023, U.S.A.

A national service organization dedicated to promoting regional ballet companies, both professional and non-vocational, throughout the U.S.A. Publishes *Dance/America* quarterly.

The Professional Children's School   132, West 60th Street, New York, N.Y. 10023, U.S.A.

The only fully accredited non-profit school in the U.S.A. offering an academic college preparatory education to young performers and those studying for careers in the arts, including dance, music and theatre students as well as those training for careers in competitive sports. The Lower School covers grades 3–8, the High School, grades 9–12, and there is also a Correspondence Programme. The School of American Ballet (the official school of New York City Ballet Co.) has a close association with the Professional Children's School.

The Dancers Resettlement Office   9, Fitzroy Square, London W1P 6AE

Administers funds for the assistance of dancers enabling them to take up new occupations at the end of their careers.

INDEX

A Chorus Line, 6, 86
adage, 32, 61, 63, 66
Alston, Richard, 35, 41, 45, 60, 64, 65
Alvin Ailey Company, The, 43
American Ballet Theatre, The, 21
American Ballet Theatre School, The, 27
American choreographers, 27
American Dance Guild, The, 110
American Dance Therapy Association, The, 109
Arpino, Gerald, 27
Arts Educational School, 52, 53
Ashton, Frederick, 20, 21
Association of Ballet Clubs, The, 111
Astaire, Fred, 16, 63
auditions, 6, 55
Augins, Charles, 48
Australian Ballet Company, The, 21, 102
Australian Ballet School, The, 102
Backstage, 55, 107
Balanchine, George, 20
ballet
  as a universal language, 19
  Australian, 21
  class, format of, 25, 27-32, 82, 83
  classical, 19
  companies, 27, 85
  French, 19, 21
  groups, 27
  history of, 14-15
  in Europe, 11-12
  Italian, 19
  Russian, 19, 21
  schools, 18, 21-26
  standards, 26, 27
  steps of elevation, 32
  student, timetable of, 32
  techniques, 19-20, 42
  training for, 1, 22, 27
  types of, 19
Ballet Bookshop, The, 110
Ballet du XX ème Siècle. *See* Béjart, Maurice.
'Ballet for All,' 85
Ballet Rambert, 23, 46, 98
'ballets de cour,' 13
Ballets Russes, 15
ballroom dancing, 94

Ballroom Faculty, 3
Barbieri, Margaret, 60, 64
'barefoot dance,' 35
Baryshnikov, Mikhail, 11, 16
batterie, 32
Bayda, Gregory, 94
beginner in dance, 2, 4-5, 39-42
Béjart, Maurice, 26, 100, 101
Benesh dance notation, 76-77, 108
Bergese, Micha, 45
blacks in dance, 27, 45-46
Blasis, Carlo, 20
bookshops, 110
Bournonville ballet, 14, 100
Bradshaw, Steve, 92
British Ballet, 98
British Ballet Organization, 2, 104
British Broadcasting Corporation, 92
Broadway, 54, 55, 58
Broomhead, Phillip, 18, 28-31, 68, 72
Bruce, Christopher, 45-46
Bubblin' Brown Sugar, 48, 56
Butcher, Rosemary, 45
Butler, John, 46
Café de Paris, 96
Cage, John, 44
Calderon, Mark, 57
California Festival Ballet, 69
Canadian National Ballet Company, 21
Cape Town Ballet Company, 103
Cape Town University Ballet School, 102
career prospects, 1, 46, 54-58, 74-78
'cavalier,' 61, 66
Cecchetti, Enrico, 15
Cecchetti Society, The, 104
Cenaiko, Marcella, 95
Centraal Dansberaad, 101
Checkmate. *See* De Valois, Ninette
Chelsea-Westminster Adult Education Institute, 90
choreography, 11, 20, 27, 39, 44-46, 50, 54, 59, 61, 70, 71, 76, 81
Choreology, 108
City of Antwerp, 100
Civic Ballets, The, 27
Class, 36-37, 40
clothes for class, 5
Coda, 66

Cohan, Robert, 36-40, 45, 46
Contact-improvisation, 43
contemporary dance. *See* modern dance
contracts, 74-75
Coppèlia, 85
corps de ballet, 61, 75, 79, 81, 84, 85
coryphees, 75, 84
costume in dance, 14, 35
Council for Dance Education and Training, The, 110
Country Dance and Song Society of America, The, 109
Cranko, John, 20
Cunningham, Merce, 43-44
Dalcroze, Emile Jaques, 108
Dalcroze eurhythmics, 7, 93, 94, 108
Dalcroze Society, The, 109
dance
  academic principles of, 20
  advice, 1-8
  as amateur theatre, 89
  as entertainment, 13-14
  as social pastime, 12-13, 94
  as therapy, 94, 109-111
  classes, 23, 24, 51-53, 57, 82, 93
  companies, 22-23, 43, 46
  conditioning, 90
  duets, 60, 66-67
  elements of, 61-62
  European, 11-17, 26-27
  for pleasure, 89
  for the beginner, 4-6
  groups, 43, 75
  historical, 91-92
  history of, 11-17, 35-38
  in education, 92-94
  lessons, 27-32
  national characteristics of, 21
  notation, 76-77
  organizations, 2-3, 109
  partners, famous, 63
  pioneers, 44
  publications, 105-106
  reasons for learning, 89-90
  rehearsals, 64-65, 83, 91
  requirements, 32
  schools, 4-6, 21-32, 38, 97-102
  specialization, 2, **14**, **63**
  standards, 74
  talent for, 4
  training for, 1-2, **49-50**
  unions, 54
Dance and Dancers, 3
'dance arrangement,' 20

Dance Books, 110
Dance Captain, 58
'Dance for People with Disabilities,' 94, 110
Dance in Canada, 111
Dance in Canada Association, 111
Dance Magazine, 3, 106
Dance Magazine Annual, 106
Dance Magazine Directory of Dance in Colleges and Universities, 92
Dance Notation Bureau, The, 108
Dance Scope, 106, 110
Dance Theatre of Harlem, 26
dancer
  as athlete, 7, 9, 90
  as principal, 75
  as soloist, 75
  daily routine of, 79-86
Dancers Resettlement Office, The, 111
Dancing Times, The, 3, 105-106
dansants, 96
Danse, 106
danse à deux, 61
danse d'école, 20
Dauberval, Jean, 11
Davie, Peter, 24
Davies, Siobhan, 45
De Valois, Ninette, 20
Diaghilev Company, 15, 104
Diaghilev, Sergei, 21
dieting, 7
dinner theatres, 55
Dolin, Anton, 63
double-work, 32, 61, 66-67, 70-72
Dowell, Anthony, 63
Duncan, Isadora, 35
Dupré, Louis, 11
Dutch National Ballet Company, 21
Ecole de Danse de l'Opera, 21, 99-100
Ecole de la Rue de Suresnes, 100
Egorova, Lubor, 105
Emblen, Ronald, 87
EMMA Dance Company, 46
employment, 26, 43
English Folk Dance and Song Society, The, 96, 109
Equity status, 54-55
Eshkol-Wachman Notation, 108
Espinosa, Edouard, 104
European dance, 11-14
examinations, for dance, 5-6

experimentation in dance, 44-45
'expressionist dance,' 35
Extemporary Dance Company, 46
Faculty of Fine Arts, The, 92
Faculty of Music, The, 92
Falco, Louis, 46
famous dancers, 11, 63
Federal National School of Australia. See Australian Ballet School.
F.I.E.R., 109
Fleming, Colin, 88, 91
Fokine, Michel, 15
folk dance, 95-96
Fonteyn, Margot, 63
Forella, Ron, 51
'free dance,' 35
French ballet, 19
French Revolution, 14
French, Vicki, 85
Giselle, 11, 20, 62
Graham, Martha, 38-39
Grand Pas de Deux Classique, 66
Greater London Council, The, 58
Harding-Irmer, 36
Harris, Duff, 69
Helpmann, Robert, 63
Here We Come, 33
Historical Dance Branch, 92
history of men in dance, 11-17
Hollywood Drama-Logue, 107
Humphrey, Doris, 43
Imperial Russian Ballet, 15, 105
Imperial Society of Teachers of Dancing, The, 2-3, 50, 92, 103-104, 110
Institute of Choreology, Ltd., 108
Institut Jaques-Dalcroze, 109
International Council of Ballroom Dancing, 109
Italian ballet, 19
jazz dance, 49-52
Jobe, Tom, 35, 46
Joffrey, Robert, 27
Johansson, Christian, 15
Joos, Kurt, 35
Juilliard School of Music, The, 38, 43
Junior Associates of the Royal Ballet School, The, 97-98
Karsavina, Tamara, 15
Kchessinska, Mathilde, 105
Kelly, Desmond, 60
Kelly, Gene, 16

kinaesthetic sympathy, 13, 17
King Louis XIV, 12, 14
Laban Centre for Movement and Dance, The, 92
Laban dance notation, 77, 108
Labanotation, 108
La Danse, 110
Legat, Nicholas, 105
Les Saisons de la Danse, 107
Lifar, Serge, 21
Limon, José, 43, 46
Line Captain. See Dance Captain.
Littlejohn, Olive, 85
London Contemporary Dance Theatre, The, 35, 36, 38-41, 43, 45, 46
London Festival Ballet, The, 23
London School for Contemporary Dance, The, 3, 98
Luigi, 51
Lycée Racine, 100
Maas Movers, 46
MacMillan, Kenneth, 21, 71
Markova, Alicia, 63
Masque of Separation, 46
Massine, Leonide, 16
Mattox, Matt, 51
Mayerling. See MacMillan, Kenneth.
May I Have the Pleasure? The Story of Popular Dancing, 92
McKim, Ross, 45
McLorg, Tamara, 45
Mercury, Freddy, 81
Mercury Theatre, 98
Ministry of Education, 101
Mitchell, Arthur, 27
modern dance, 16-17, 35-46
Modern Stage Dance, 50
Morgan, Elizabeth, 65
Morrice, Norman, 46
Morris dancing, 92
Mudra. See Béjart, Maurice
Municipal Ballet Institute, The, 100
Municipal Opera, The, 54
musical training, 7
Must Wear Tights, 59
Myths about men in dance, 9-11
Natasha Lisakova School of Dance, 95
National Association for Regional Ballet, The, 109, 110
National Ballet School of Canada, 33

113

National Council of Dance Teachers Organizations, The, 109
'natural dance,' 96
New Dance, 16, 35, 107
New York City Ballet, 20
New York City Ballet Company, 22, 99
Nijinsky, Vaslav, 15-16, 104
Nikolais, Alwin, 44-45
Northern Ballet Theatre, 23
North, Robert, 45, 46
notation, methods of, 108
Noverre, Jean Georges, 11
Nureyev, Rudolf, 11, 16, 63
Olga Fricker School, 57
operatic dancing, 104
Paris Opera Ballet, The, 21-22
Paris Opera, The, 14, 46
partners, 32, 61-72
pas de deux, 32, 60-61, 63, 68, 71
Pavlova, Anna, 15, 104
Paxton, Steve, 43
Peden, David, 65
Petipa-Tchaikowsky classics, 21
physical requirements for dance, 26
Pilobolus Dance Theatre, 45
Pineapple Poll. See Cranko, John.
pirouettes, 32
Place, The. See London School of Contemporary Dance.
plié, 19
pointes, 11, 62, 63
premier danseur, 66
Preobajenska, Olga, 105
prima ballerina, 66
Professional Children's School, The, 99, 111
Queen Elizabeth II Art Council of New Zealand, 102
Quirey, Belinda, 92
Rainbow Bandit, 35, 41
Rake's Progress, The, 24
Rambert Academy, 9
Rambert School of Ballet, 98
'resting,' 49

Robbins, Jerome, 20
Robert Joffrey Company, 46
Roberts, Nicola, 66, 72
Rock dance, 92
Rogers, Ginger, 63
Roseland, 96
Royal Academy of Dancing, 2, 5, 103
Royal Ballet, The, 21, 82, 83
Royal Ballet Choreographic Group, The, 81
Royal Ballet Company, The, 79-80, 85-86
Royal Ballet School, The, 3, 18, 21-24, 64-65, 68, 80, 97
Royal Danish Ballet, The 22
Royal Danish Ballet School, The, 100
Royal Opera House, The, 22, 79-81, 85, 87
Russian ballet, 19
Russian Imperial Ballet, 15-16
Russian Revival, 14-16
Sadler's Wells Royal Ballet, 60, 83
Sadler's Wells Theatre, 41
School, The. See Rambert Academy.
School of American Ballet, The, 22, 27, 99
Scottish Ballet, 23
Scottish Country Dance Society, The, 96, 109
sexuality in dance, 9-11
Shawn, Ted, 16, 35
Sheriff, Stephen, 79-82, 84-86
shoes for dance, 4-5
showbusiness, 49-59, 72, 75
Sibley, Antoinette, 63
Sinfonietta, 64, 65
Sleeping Beauty, The, 20, 79
Smedley, Ronald, 92
Smith, Janet, 45
Society for Russian Style Ballet, The, 104
Sokolow, Anna, 46
Somes, Michael, 63, 79
Spink, Ian, 45
Squires, Dougie, 59
Stage and Television Today, The, 55

Standard Equity Overseas Contract, 55
St. Denis, Ruth, 35
Stedelijk Instituut voor Ballet. See Municipal Ballet Institute
Sutton Notation, 108
Summer Stock, 54
sur les pointes, 11, 62
Symphonic Variation. See Ashton, Frederick.
Taylor, Paul, 43, 46
Tchaikowsky, Peter Ilich, 15
teachers, 3, 11, 24, 51, 77, 108
teaching associations, 103-105
courses, 105
Tetley, Glen, 46, 72
Tharp, Twyla, 45-46
Theatre Faculty, 2-3
theatrical presentations, amateur, 90
Time Out, 107
Tokyo Ballet, 78
tours, 32
training, 25, 27
Travolta, John, 16-17
Two Pigeons, The, 60, 64
United States Ballroom Branch of the Imperial Society of Teachers of Dancing, 109
Vaganova, Agrippina, 105
Vestris, Gaetano and Auguste, 11
Village Voice, The, 107
Von Laban, Rudolf, 35, 94
Walker, William, 53
Weaver, John, 11
Weidman, Charles, 43
West London Institute of Higher Education, 98
Westminster Morris Men, 88, 91
Whitgate Nursery School, 93
Wigman, Mary, 35
Winter Stock, 55
working conditions, 54-58, 74-78
X6 Dance Collective, 45-46
Zerbe, Jennet, 69
Zerebecky, Bohdan, 95